W9-BPM-970

Selections from the
BLACK

Book Two

Provocative Selections by Black Writers

College Reading Skills

JAMESTOWN PUBLISHERS

a division of NTC/CONTEMPORARY PUBLISHING GROUP
Lincolnwood, Illinois USA

Books in the *Selections from the Black* Series

Book One   Book Three
Book Two   Book Four

ON THE COVER

The art shown on the cover of this book is *Black Sea Rising* by Derric Clemmons, a sculptor-writer-illustrator. The work, done in acrylic and latex, is a view of the October 1995 Million Man March in Washington, D.C.

Clemmons was born in Chicago in 1962. He attended Columbia College and in 1984 studied in Europe with an Italian artist. Clemmons has continued to develop his work and has gained recognition through exhibitions around Chicago.

He describes the cover painting as a "fractalization" of cubism and expressionism. "It is a blending of environment and emotional response to the human condition," Clemmons explains. His recent work reflects this view from an urbanized perspective.

Editorial Director: Cynthia Krejcsi

Executive Editor: Marilyn Cunningham

Associate Editor: Lisa Abel

Editorial Services Manager: Sylvia Bace

Market Development Manager: Tana McDonald

Design Manager: Ophelia M. Chambliss

Production Manager: Margo Goia

Acknowledgments, which are on the facing page, are considered an extension of this copyright page.

ISBN: 0-89061-840-2
Published by Jamestown Publishers,
a division of NTC/Contemporary Publishing Group, Inc.,
4255 West Touhy Avenue,
Lincolnwood (Chicago), Illinois 60712-1975, U.S.A.
©1998 by NTC/Contemporary Publishing Group, Inc.
All rights reserved. No part of this publication may be reproduced,
stored in a retrieval system, or transmitted in any form or by any means,
electronic, mechanical, photocopying, recording, or otherwise,
without the prior permission of the Publisher.

Manufactured in the United States of America.

5 6 7 8 9 10 11 12 021 09 08 07 06 05 04

ACKNOWLEDGMENTS

Acknowledgment is gratefully made to the following publishers, authors, and agents for permission to reprint these works. Every effort has been made to determine copyright owners. In the case of any omissions, the Publisher will be pleased to make suitable acknowledgments in future editions.

"Go Tell It on the Mountain." Text excerpt from *Go Tell It on the Mountain* by James Baldwin. Copyright © 1952, 1953 by James Baldwin. Reprinted by permission of Doubleday, a division of Bantam Doubleday Dell Publishing Group, Inc.

"'Taint So." Text excerpt from *Something in Common* by Langston Hughes. Copyright © 1963 by Langston Hughes. Copyright renewed © 1991 by Arnold Rampersad and Ramona Bass. Reprinted by permission of Hill and Wang, a division of Farrar, Straus & Giroux, Inc.

"Jazz." Text excerpt from *Jazz* by Toni Morrison. Copyright © 1992 by Alfred A. Knopf. Reprinted by permission of International Creative Management, Inc.

"Die Nigger Die!" Text excerpt from *Die Nigger Die!* by H. Rap Brown. Copyright © 1969 by Lynne Brown. Reprinted by permission of Doubleday, a division of Bantam Doubleday Dell Publishing Group, Inc.

"The Autobiography of Malcolm X." Text excerpt from *The Autobiography of Malcolm X* by Malcolm X with the assistance of Alex Haley. Copyright 1965 © by Alex Haley and Betty Shabazz. Reprinted by permission of Random House, Inc.

"The Women of Brewster Place." Text excerpt from "Mattie Michael," from *The Women of Brewster Place* by Gloria Naylor. Copyright © 1980, 1982 by Gloria Naylor. Reprinted by permission of Viking Penguin, a division of Penguin Books USA, Inc.

"My American Journey." Text excerpt from *My American Journey* by Colin L. Powell with Joseph E. Persico. Copyright © 1995 by Colin L. Powell. Reprinted by permission of Random House, Inc.

"The Autobiography of My Mother." Text excerpt from *The Autobiography of My Mother* by Jamaica Kincaid. Copyright © 1996 by Jamaica Kincaid. Reprinted by permission of Farrar, Straus & Giroux, Inc.

"The Heart of a Woman." Text excerpt from *The Heart of a Woman* by Maya Angelou. Copyright © 1981 by Maya Angelou. Reprinted by permission of Random House, Inc.

"Anticipation." Text reprint of "Anticipation" by Mabel Dove-Danquah from *An African Treasury*, edited by Langston Hughes, 1960. Published by Crown Publishers, Inc.

"Bloods." Text excerpt from *Bloods* by Wallace Terry. Copyright © 1984 by Wallace Terry. Reprinted by permission of Random House, Inc.

"Showing My Color." Text excerpt from Chapter 6, "Resistance Motifs," from *Showing My Color: Impolite Essays on Race and Identity* by Clarence Page. Copyright © 1996 by Clarence Page. Reprinted by permission of HarperCollins Publishers, Inc.

"Let the Trumpet Sound." Text excerpt from *Let the Trumpet Sound: The Life of Martin Luther King, Jr.* by Stephen B. Oates. Copyright © 1982, 1994 by Stephen B. Oates. Reprinted by permission of HarperCollins Publishers, Inc.

"A Man's Life." Text excerpt from *A Man's Life: An Autobiography* by Roger Wilkins. Copyright © 1982 by Roger Wilkins, published by Simon & Schuster, Inc. Reprinted by permission of Roger Wilkins.

"Showing His True Colors." Text reprint of "Showing His True Colors" by Angela Bouwsma, *Newsweek*, February 24, 1997. All rights reserved. Reprinted by permission.

"The Dark Child." Text excerpt from *The Dark Child* by Camara Laye, translated by James Kirkup, Ernest Jones, and Elaine Gottlieb. Copyright © 1954 and renewed © 1982 by Camara Laye. Reprinted by permission of Hill and Wang, a division of Farrar, Straus & Giroux, Inc.

"The Harlem Rat." Text excerpt from "The Harlem Rat" by John H. Jones in *Harlem, U.S.A.*, edited by John Henrik Clarke. Published in 1964 by Seven Sea Publications.

Author Photographs

James Baldwin: Jack Manning/New York Times/Archive Photos; Langston Hughes: J. Sommer Coll/Archive Photos; Toni Morrison: Christopher Felver/Archive Photos; Booker T. Washington: Archive Photos; H. Rap Brown: Archive Photos; Frederick Douglass: Archive Photos; Malcolm X: Archive Photos; Gloria Naylor: Marion Ettlinger; Colin Powell: Archive Photos/Victor Malafronte; Jamaica Kincaid: Mariana Cook; Maya Angelou: Stephen Matteson, Jr./New York Times/Archive Photos; Clarence Page: Ernie Cox, Jr.

CONTENTS

1 Introductory Selection

EXPLAINS HOW THE TEXT IS ORGANIZED AND HOW TO USE IT TO MAXIMUM ADVANTAGE

VOCABULARY, PART ONE—

All of these terms are in the selection you are about to read. Study each term and its meaning. Then answer the questions below.

As you read the story, notice how each term is used. You will have more questions about the terms later.

intent, purpose

moderate, calm; avoiding extremes

intervening, coming between

oppression, persecution; great hardship

servitude, a lack of freedom; slavery

efficient, able to perform a task easily and skillfully

consecutively, coming one after another in order

corresponding, matching

diagnostic, helping to analyze or find problems

discriminating, able to see differences and distinctions

1

1. If you counted from 1 to 100 in order, how would you be presenting the numbers?

    _____

2. Which term would you use if you were talking about the years between, for example, 1968 and 1991? _____

3. Which term could describe a person who works without wasting any effort?

    _____

4. Which term would describe a person who could easily tell the difference between real and fake emeralds? _____

5. Which term could describe a person who takes a middle-of-the-road position on various issues? _____

A READING PURPOSE—

The following passage will tell you something about the selections in this book and how each chapter is structured. As you read, decide which chapter part will be most helpful to you to improve your reading.

(Before you begin reading this selection, turn to page 4 and record the hours and minutes in the box labeled Starting Time at the bottom of the second column. If you are using this text in class and your instructor has made provisions for timing, you need not stop now; read on.)

■

You are using this text for two purposes: (1) to improve your reading and study skills and (2) to read what black people are saying now and what they have said in the past.

Over 20 years ago, when *Selections from the Black* was first published, our nation was just beginning to realize that blacks had a voice and had something to say. The publisher's intent was to assemble selections from black writers and publish them so that our texts might racially balance the other literature that college students were expected to read. When these texts were first published, there were objections from those who felt that a menu of exclusively black writings only served to further isolate African-American students from the American mainstream.

Fortunately, moderate thought prevailed, and the concept of a black reading and study skills program was accepted. In the intervening years tens of thousands of students, black and white, have used *Selections from the Black* with satisfaction and success.

In the selections in this series, you will read the words of slaves describing their days of oppression. You will read the words of yesterday's leaders—DuBois, Garvey, Washington, and others—and begin to understand the history and background of Negro servitude. You will understand how the thinking of these writers influenced their times and ours.

You will read the words of authors from the more recent past, describing the explosive racial climate of the 1950s and 1960s. This text presents the voices of protest, moderate and defiant, including those silenced by death, exile, and imprisonment. Writers of both extremes are presented here because their words have structured and defined black America.

You will also read selections representing the black experience in the 1980s and 1990s, and from these you will get some idea of the way their authors feel life has—and has not—changed. The works of African and Caribbean writers are included as well, including some that deal with South Africa's longstanding white-minority rule and policy of apartheid. These messages from South Africa are important to us because apartheid was long an issue of international proportions and forms a significant part of the total black experience.

Black men and women writing about politics, sports, business, journalism, and entertainment have contributed to this series. Also included are many master writers of fiction; their stories, rich with feeling, are part of the treasury of black literature.

We want you to enjoy these selections, and we want you to learn from them. We especially want you to understand the situation of the black person over time and throughout history.

The other purpose for using this text, that of reading and study improvement, recognizes reality too: the reality of today. This text will help you to develop skills and techniques necessary for efficiency in our society.

Included with each selection is a Study Skills exercise. In these exercises you will learn methods of understanding, critical thinking skills, techniques of comprehension, and many other key ways to improve your reading ability. The Study Skills exercises are designed to assist you in developing efficient reading techniques. As you read the selections in this book, you will find that often one Study Skills exercise leads directly to the next. It is important to read and work the Study Skills exercises consecutively in order to understand fully each subject.

Today's reader must be flexible enough to choose from a supply of skills one that is suitable for each reading task. The skilled reader has learned that each kind of reading matter demands a corresponding reading technique—there is no single "best" way to read. As you complete the selections and exercises in this book, you will find your reading skills growing.

USING THE TEXT

The 20 selections are designed to be read in numerical order, starting with the Introductory Selection and ending with Selection 20. Because the selections increase in difficulty as you progress through the book, the earlier ones prepare you to handle the upcoming ones successfully.

Here are the procedures to follow for reading each selection.

1. Read the Author Notes.
At the beginning of each chapter is a brief biography of the selection's author. This biography will make you familiar with the time and place in which the author was writing as well as his or her special accomplishments and concerns. Reading the biography will help you get more out of the selection.

2. Answer the Vocabulary Questions.
Immediately preceding each selection is a vocabulary previewing activity. The activity includes 10 vocabulary words from the selection, their meanings as they are used in the selection, and 5 questions related to those words. To answer each question, you will choose from and write one of the 10 vocabulary words. Previewing the vocabulary in such a fashion will give you a head start on understanding the words when you encounter them in the selection. The words are underlined for easy reference.

3. Preview Before Reading.
Previewing acquaints you with the overall content and structure of the selection before you actually read. It is like consulting a road map before taking a trip: planning the route gives you more confidence as you proceed and, perhaps, helps you avoid any unnecessary delays. Previewing should take about a minute or two and is done in this way:
   a)   Read the title. Learn the writer's subject and, possibly, his or her point of view on it.
   b)   Read the opening and closing paragraphs. These contain the introductory and concluding remarks. Important information is frequently presented in these key paragraphs.
   c)   Skim through. Try to discover the author's approach to the subject. Does he or she use many examples? Is the writer's purpose to convince you about certain ideas? What else can you learn now to help you when you read?

4. Establish a Reading Purpose.
After you have previewed the selection, establish a purpose for reading the selection. Use the suggestion that precedes the selection; it will help you complete some of the later activities.

5. Read the Selection.
Do not try to race through. Read well and carefully enough so that you can answer the comprehension questions that follow.

Keep track of your reading time by noting when you start and finish. A table on page 122 converts your reading time to a words-per-minute rate. Select the time from the table that is closest to your reading time. Record those figures in the boxes at the end of the selection. Be aware that there is no one ideal reading speed for everything. The efficient reader varies reading speed as the selection requires.

Many of the selections have been reprinted from full-length books and novels. If you find a particular selection interesting, you may enjoy reading the entire book. Complete information is contained in a bibliography on page 121.

> "It is important to understand the situation of the black person over time and throughout history."

6. Answer the Comprehension Questions.

After you have read the selection, find the comprehension questions that follow. These have been included to test your understanding of what you have read. The questions are <u>diagnostic</u> too. Because the comprehension skill being measured is identified, you can detect your areas of weakness.

Read each question carefully and, without looking back, select one of the four choices given that answers that question most accurately or most completely. Frequently all four choices, or options, given for a question are *correct*, but one is the *best* answer. For this reason some comprehension questions are highly challenging and require you to be highly <u>discriminating</u>. You may, from time to time, disagree with an answer. When this happens, you have an opportunity to sharpen your powers of discrimination. Study the question again and seek to discover why the listed answer may be best. When you disagree with the text, you are thinking; when you objectively analyze and recognize your errors, you are learning.

A profitable habit for you to acquire is the practice of analyzing the questions you have answered incorrectly. If time permits, return to the selection to find and underline the passages containing the correct answers. This process helps you to see what you missed the first time. Some interpretive and generalization-type questions are not answered specifically in the text. In these cases bracket the parts of the selections that refer to the correct answers. Your instructor may recommend that you complete this step outside of class as homework.

7. Answer Additional Vocabulary Questions.

Following the comprehension section are two sets of sentences using the 10 vocabulary words introduced earlier. Each fill-in-the-blank sentence requires you to choose the correct word after looking at the context (surrounding words). This format gives you an opportunity to improve your ability to use context as an aid in understanding words. The efficient use of context is a valuable vocabulary tool.

The boxes following the vocabulary activity contain space for your comprehension scores and your scores from this second vocabulary activity. Each correct vocabulary item is worth 10 points, and each correct comprehension answer is worth 10 points.

Pages 123 and 124 contain graphs to be used for plotting your scores and tallying your incorrect responses. On page 123 record your comprehension score at the appropriate intersection of lines, using an X. Use a circle or some other mark on the same graph to record your vocabulary results. Some students prefer to use different color inks or pencil and ink to distinguish between comprehension and vocabulary plottings.

On page 124 darken the squares to indicate the comprehension questions you have missed. By referring to the Skills Profile as you progress through the text, you and your instructor will be able to tell which questions give you the most trouble. As soon as you detect a specific weakness in comprehension, consult with your instructor to see what supplementary materials he or she can provide or suggest.

8. Write About the Selection.

A brief writing activity allows you to offer your own opinions about some aspect of the selection. Here you are always asked to write a few clearly written paragraphs, containing as many specific facts or examples as possible, to complete each writing assignment.

9. Complete the Study Skills Exercises.

Concluding each chapter is a passage on study skills, followed by five completion questions to be answered after you have finished the passage. One or two of these questions will always ask you to apply the study skill to the selection you have just read.

If class time is at a premium, your instructor may prefer that you complete some or all of these activities out of class.

All of the selections in this text are structured just like this introductory one. After completing this selection and its exercises, you will be prepared to proceed to Selection 2.

Starting Time ☐

Reading Time ☐

Finishing Time ☐

■ Reading Rate ☐

COMPREHENSION —

Read the following questions and statements. For each one, put an X in the box before
the option that contains the most complete or accurate answer.

1. How much time should you devote to previewing a selection?
   - ☐ a. Your time will vary with each selection.
   - ☐ b. You should devote about one or two minutes to previewing.
   - ☐ c. No specific time is suggested.
   - ☐ d. None—the instructor times the selection.

2. The way the vocabulary exercises are described suggests that
   - ☐ a. the meaning of a word often depends on how it is used.
   - ☐ b. the final authority for word meaning is the dictionary.
   - ☐ c. words have precise and permanent meanings.
   - ☐ d. certain words are always difficult to understand.

3. The writer of this passage presents the facts in order of
   - ☐ a. importance.
   - ☐ b. purpose.
   - ☐ c. time.
   - ☐ d. occurrence.

4. *Selections from the Black* is based on which of the following premises?
   - ☐ a. Literature for college students needed to be racially balanced.
   - ☐ b. Black students learn best from black writers.
   - ☐ c. The writings of black authors should provoke student interest.
   - ☐ d. Traditional reading improvement tests are racially unfair.

5. How does the writer feel about reading speed?
   - ☐ a. It is a minimal aspect of the total reading situation.
   - ☐ b. It is second (following comprehension) in the ranking of skills.
   - ☐ c. It will vary from selection to selection.
   - ☐ d. It should be developed at an early age.

6. The introductory selection
   - ☐ a. eliminates the need for oral instruction.
   - ☐ b. permits the student to learn by doing.
   - ☐ c. explains the proper use of the text in detail.
   - ☐ d. allows for variety and interest.

7. The introductory selection suggests that
   - ☐ a. most readers are not flexible.
   - ☐ b. students should learn to use different reading skills for different types of reading matter.
   - ☐ c. students today read better than students of the past did.
   - ☐ d. 20 selections is an ideal number for a reading improvement text.

8. The overall tone of this passage is
   - ☐ a. serious.
   - ☐ b. suspenseful.
   - ☐ c. humorous.
   - ☐ d. sarcastic.

9. The author of this selection is probably
   - ☐ a. a doctor.
   - ☐ b. an accountant.
   - ☐ c. an educator.
   - ☐ d. a businessman.

10. The writer of this passage makes his point clear by
    - ☐ a. telling a story.
    - ☐ b. listing historical facts.
    - ☐ c. using metaphors.
    - ☐ d. giving directions.

Comprehension Skills

1. recalling specific facts
2. retaining concepts
3. organizing facts
4. understanding the main idea
5. drawing a conclusion
6. making a judgment
7. making an inference
8. recognizing tone
9. understanding characters
10. appreciating literary forms

VOCABULARY, PART TWO —

Write the term that makes the most sense in each
sentence.

oppression   intervening
efficient   intent
consecutively

1. The purpose of this book was never to isolate black
   writers; instead, its _____ was
   to make them a part of the total curriculum.

2. The _____ years between the first publication of this book and the present have shown that the author's idea was correct.

3. Many of the writers represented in this book suffered _____ .

4. Because the study skills are presented in order, it is important to study each chapter _____ .

5. By applying the study skills as you go, you will become a more _____ reader.

moderate	diagnostic
discriminating	corresponding
servitude	

6. Besides slavery, the writers in this book had to endure other types of _____ .

7. Responses of the writers to discrimination ranged from _____ to extreme.

8. Mark the box _____ to the right response for each comprehension question.

9. You must be especially _____ between possible answers for some questions.

10. You can use your wrong answers in a _____ way to figure out your reading weaknesses.

Comprehension Score [   ]

Vocabulary Score [   ]

W R I T I N G —

Think about the weaknesses you might have as a reader. In what ways do you think the chapters in this book will be most helpful in overcoming them? Write a few paragraphs explaining what you think. Be as specific as you can.

S T U D Y S K I L L S —

Read the following passage and answer the questions that follow it.

Paragraphs of Introduction

Like other prose writers, textbook authors present their ideas in paragraphs. The effectiveness of their communication with readers depends on how well they have structured those paragraphs.

A writer begins with an introductory paragraph. Like a speaker, a writer offers remarks to open the discussion of a topic. Speakers often tell a story or two to "warm up" listeners, but writers are not face to face with their audience, and must do more to get the readers ready. Recognizing this limitation of communication through the printed page, writers stive to create an effective opening with which to introduce their topic to the readers.

The opening paragraph is called the paragraph of introduction; it serves as an announcement of what is to come. Writers may state the purpose they hope to accomplish in the following paragraphs, offer a brief outline of their major concepts, or mention one or two ideas the reader will encounter later in the piece.

Because a paragraph of introduction offers a preview of what will follow, it is especially useful when previewing a selection. In magazine articles and similar reading material, the introductory paragraph must capture the reader's interest with just a few words. Readers can expect any of a variety of interest-compelling devices that a skilled writer may employ for this purpose.

1. To communicate effectively, textbook authors depend on well-structured _____ .

2. Recognizing their limits within the _____ , writers must try to create an effective way to introduce the subject to the reader.

3. The paragraph of introduction is used as a sort of _____ of things to come.

4. The paragraph of introduction in this selection cites two _____ for using this textbook.

5. One of those has two parts: to improve reading and _____ skills.

6

2

Go Tell It on the Mountain

James Baldwin

AUTHOR NOTES—
Novelist and essayist James Baldwin was born in 1924 in New York City. The first of nine children, he grew up in Harlem, where his father was a minister. When he was 24, Baldwin left the United States for a 10-year stay in Europe. Residing mainly in Paris, he wrote and published his first three books. In 1957 Baldwin returned to the United States to join the civil rights struggle. For the next several years he divided his time between a home in southern France and one in New York City. He then returned to Europe permanently, where he died in 1987.

Baldwin's published works include, among others, his semiautobiographical first novel, *Go Tell It on the Mountain*, as well as *Another Country*, a novel examining racial and sexual issues, and the essay collection *Notes of a Native Son*. He also achieved recognition for two plays, *Blues for Mister Charlie* and *The Amen Corner*. His stories and essays have appeared in many magazines both here and abroad.

VOCABULARY, PART ONE—

All of these terms are in the story you are about to read. Study each term and its meaning. Then answer the questions below.

As you read the story, notice how each term is used. You will have more questions about the terms later.

hysterical, extremely upset; out of control

approximate, to imitate closely

threshold, doorstep; place or point of entering

ceased, stopped

anguish, grief; sorrow

improvised, done quickly without preparation

intentness, earnestness; determination

malice, a feeling of hatred, spite, or ill will

vindictive, revengeful; holding a grudge

pathetic, arousing pity

1. Which term could describe a speech you gave without writing it in advance?

   _____

2. Which term would describe the feelings of a person who hates his neighbor and wishes bad things for him? _____

3. If you had just stopped smoking, what would be another term for saying you quit?

   _____

4. Which term would describe a person who wants to get back at someone who has gotten her fired? _____

5. What would you call the entrance to the front of a house?

   _____

A READING PURPOSE—

This selection describes a stressful family event. As you read, decide what you think of the relationship between John and his father.

_____

■

1 As John approached his home again in the late afternoon, he saw little Sarah, her coat unbuttoned, come flying out of the house and run the length of the street away from him into the far drugstore. Instantly, he was frightened; he stopped a moment, staring blankly down the street, wondering what could justify such <u>hysterical</u> haste. It was true that Sarah was full of self-importance, and made any errand she ran seem a matter of life or death; nevertheless, she had been sent on an errand, and with such speed that her mother had not had time to make her button up her coat.

2 Then he felt weary; if something really happened it would be very unpleasant upstairs now, and he did not want to face it. But perhaps it was simply that his mother had a headache and had sent Sarah to the store for some aspirin. But if this were true, it meant that he would have to prepare supper, and take care of the children, and be naked under his father's eyes all the evening long. And he began to walk more slowly.

3 There were some boys standing on the stoop. They watched him as he approached, and he tried not to look at them and to <u>approximate</u> the swagger with which they walked. One of them said, as he mounted the short, stone steps and started into the hall: "Boy, your brother was hurt real bad today."

4 He looked at them in a kind of dread, not daring to ask for details; and he observed that they, too, looked as though they had been in a battle; something hangdog in their looks suggested that they had been put to flight. Then he looked down, and saw that there was blood at the <u>threshold</u>, and blood spattered on the tile floor of the vestibule. He looked again at the boys, who had not <u>ceased</u> to watch him, and hurried up the stairs.

5 The door was half open—for Sarah's return, no doubt—and he walked in, making no sound, feeling a confused impulse to flee. There was no one in the kitchen, though the light was burning—the lights were on all through the house. On the kitchen table stood a shopping-bag filled with groceries, and he knew that his Aunt Florence had arrived. The washtub, where his mother had been washing earlier, was still open, and filled the kitchen with a sour smell.

6 There were drops of blood on the floor here too, and there had been small, smudged coins of blood on the stairs as he walked up.

7 All this frightened him terribly. He stood in the middle of the kitchen, trying to imagine what had happened, and preparing himself to walk into the living room, where all the family seemed to be. Roy had been in trouble before, but this new trouble seemed to be the beginning of the fulfillment of a prophecy. He took off his coat, dropping it on a chair, and was about to start into the living-room when he heard Sarah running up the steps.

8

8 He waited, and she burst through the door, carrying a clumsy parcel.

9 "What happened?" he whispered.

10 She stared at him in astonishment, and a certain wild joy. He thought again that he really did not like his sister. Catching her breath, she blurted out, triumphantly: "Roy got stabbed with a knife!" and rushed into the living-room.

11 Roy got stabbed with a knife. Whatever this meant, it was sure that his father would be at his worst tonight. John walked slowly into the living-room.

12 His father and mother, a small basin of water between them, knelt by the sofa where Roy lay, and his father was washing the blood from Roy's forehead. It seemed that his mother, whose touch was so much more gentle, had been thrust aside by his father, who could not bear to have anyone else touch his wounded son. And now she watched, one hand in the water, the other, in a kind of <u>anguish</u>, at her waist, which was circled still by the <u>improvised</u> apron of the morning. Her face, as she watched, was full of pain and fear, of tension barely supported, and of pity that could scarcely have been expressed had she filled all the world with her weeping. His father muttered sweet, delirious things to Roy, and his hands, when he dipped them again in the basin and wrung out the cloth, were trembling. Aunt Florence, still wearing her hat and carrying her handbag, stood a little removed, looking down at them with a troubled, terrible face.

13 Then Sarah bounded into the room before him, and his mother looked up, reached out for the package, and saw him. She said nothing, but she looked at him with a strange, quick <u>intentness</u>, almost as though there were a warning on her tongue which at the moment she did not dare to utter. His Aunt Florence looked up, and said: "We been wondering where you was, boy. This bad brother of yours done gone out and got hisself hurt."

14 But John understood from her tone that the fuss was possibly, a little greater than the danger—Roy was not, after all, going to die. And his heart lifted a little. Then his father turned and looked at him.

15 "Where you been, boy," he shouted, "all this time? Don't you know you's needed here at home?"

16 More than his words, his face caused John to stiffen instantly with <u>malice</u> and fear. His father's face was terrible in anger, but now there was more than anger in it. John saw now what he had never seen there before, except in his own <u>vindictive</u> fantasies: a kind of wild, weeping terror that made the face seem younger, and yet at the same time unutterably

> Some wounds are big and showy—the whole neighborhood knows about them. Other wounds, like John's, are secrets kept in the heart.

older and more cruel. And John knew, in the moment his father's eyes swept over him, that he hated John because John was not lying on the sofa where Roy lay. John could scarcely meet his father's eyes and yet, briefly, he did, saying nothing, feeling in his heart an odd sensation of triumph, and hoping in his heart that Roy, to bring his father low, would die.

17 His mother had unwrapped the package and was opening a bottle of peroxide. "Here," she said, "you better wash it with this now." Her voice was calm and dry; she looked at his father briefly, her face unreadable, as she handed him the bottle and the cotton.

18 "This going to hurt," his father said—in such a different voice, so sad and tender!—turning again to the sofa. "But you just be a little man and hold still; it ain't going to take long."

19 John watched and listened, hating him. Roy began to moan. Aunt Florence moved to the mantel-piece and put her handbag down near the metal serpent. From the room behind him, John heard the baby begin to whimper.

20 "John," said his mother, "go and pick her up like a good boy." Her hands, which were not trembling, were still busy: she had opened the bottle of iodine and was cutting up strips of bandage.

21 John walked into his parents' bedroom and picked up the squalling baby, who was wet. The moment Ruth felt him lift her up she stopped crying and stared at him with a wide-eyed, <u>pathetic</u> stare, as though she knew that there was trouble in the house. John laughed at her so ancient-seeming distress—he was very fond of his baby sister—and whispered in her ear as he started back to the living-room: "Now, you let your big brother tell you something, baby. Just as soon as you's able to stand on your feet, you run away from *this* house, run far away." He did not quite know why he said this, or where he wanted her to run, but it made him feel instantly better.

22 His father was saying, as John came back into the room: "I'm sure going to be having some questions to ask you in a minute, old lady. I'm going to be wanting to know just how come you let this boy go out and get half killed."

23 "Oh, no, you ain't," said Aunt Florence. "You ain't going to be starting none of that mess this evening.

You know right doggone well that Roy don't never ask *nobody* if he can do *nothing*—he just go right ahead and do like he pleases. Elizabeth sure can't put no ball and chain on him. She got her hands full right here in this house, and it ain't her fault if Roy got a head just as hard as his father's."

24 "You got a awful lot to say, look like for once you could keep from putting your mouth in my business." He said this without looking at her.

25 "It ain't my fault," she said, "that you was born a fool, and always done been a fool, and ain't never going to change. I swear to my Father you'd try the patience of Job."

26 "I done told you before," he said—he had not ceased working over the moaning Roy, and was preparing now to dab the wound with iodine—"that I didn't want you coming in here and using that gutter language in front of my children."

27 "Don't you worry about my language, brother," she said with spirit, "you better start worrying about your *life*. What these children hear ain't going to do

28 them near as much harm as what they *see*."

28 "What they *see*," his father muttered, "is a poor man trying to serve the Lord. *That's* my life."

29 "Then I guarantee *you*," she said, "that they going to do their best to keep it from being *their* life. *You* mark my words."

30 He turned and looked at her, and intercepted the look that passed between the two women. John's mother, for reasons that were not at all his father's reasons, wanted Aunt Florence to keep still. He looked away, ironically. John watched his mother's mouth tighten bitterly as she dropped her eyes. His father, in silence, began bandaging Roy's forehead.

Starting Time	
Reading Time	
Finishing Time	
Reading Rate	

COMPREHENSION —

Read the following questions and statements. For each one, put an X in the box before the option that contains the most complete or accurate answer.

1. Roy was John's
   ☐ a. classmate.
   ☐ b. friend.
   ☐ c. cousin.
   ☒ d. brother.

2. In the neighborhood Roy was known as a
   ☐ a. pusher.
   ☐ b. leader.
   ☒ c. troublemaker.
   ☐ d. hustler.

3. When was Roy stabbed?
   ☒ a. before the story opened
   ☐ b. as soon as the story opened
   ☐ c. in the middle of the story
   ☐ d. at the end of the story

4. The main point of the story is to show
   ☐ a. how John and his family earned a living.
   ☒ b. that John was bitter about his family life.
   ☐ c. where most black people are forced to live.
   ☐ d. the many different feelings of people living in poverty.

5. The relationship between John and his father can be described as
   ☐ a. normal.
   ☐ b. casual.
   ☒ c. troubled.
   ☐ d. bold.

6. John reveals his personal plans for the future when he
   ☐ a. expresses his dislike for Sarah.
   ☐ b. dreads facing his father.
   ☐ c. sympathizes with his mother.
   ☒ d. whispers in Ruth's ear.

7. Roy was probably injured in
   ☐ a. an encounter with the police.
   ☐ b. a family argument.
   ☒ c. a gang fight.
   ☐ d. a grocery store robbery.

8. The atmosphere in John's house was
   ☐ a. warm.
   ☐ b. religious.
   ☒ c. uneasy.
   ☐ d. restless.

9. John's father sees himself mainly as
   - ☐ a. a responsible citizen.
   - ☐ b. a misunderstood husband.
   - ☐ c. a good provider.
   - ☑ d. a man of the Lord.

10. The statement that John's "heart lifted a little" means that he felt
   - ☐ a. arrogance.
   - ☐ b. pride.
   - ☐ c. despair.
   - ☐ d. hope.

Comprehension Skills
1. recalling specific facts
2. retaining concepts
3. organizing facts
4. understanding the main idea
5. drawing a conclusion
6. making a judgment
7. making an inference
8. recognizing tone
9. understanding characters
10. appreciating literary forms

V O C A B U L A R Y ,   P A R T   T W O —
Write the term that makes the most sense in each sentence.

anguish   **hysterical**
threshold   **ceased**
malice

1. John came to the ___threshold___ of the house and uneasily opened the door.

2. His sister had sounded ___hysterical___, as if she were totally out of control.

3. The boys on the street hated Roy and spoke of him with _____.

4. When John entered the house, everyone quieted down and ___ceased___ talking.

5. The sorrowful look on his mother's face revealed the _____ she felt.

approximate   intentness
vindictive   pathetic
improvised

6. John felt sorry for his mother because she seemed so _____.

7. She had _____ a hospital bed for Roy by spreading blankets on the sofa.

8. John's look of _____ after he spoke to his baby sister showed that he had made up his mind about something.

9. His father was _____ enough to want to go after whoever had injured Roy.

10. John did not want to _____ his father's approach to life; he had his own ideas about how to live.

Comprehension Score [   ]

Vocabulary Score [   ]

W R I T I N G —
What are John's feelings about his father? What things about his father make John feel the way he does? Write a few paragraphs explaining John's feelings and his reasons for them. Use examples from the story to support the points you make.

S T U D Y   S K I L L S —
Read the following passage and answer the questions that follow it.

Paragraphs of Illustration
As the name suggests, paragraphs of illustration present examples, illustrations, stories, anecdotes, and so on. They are used by the author to illustrate, clarify, demonstrate, or amplify some idea or concept for the reader. Authors use many paragraphs of illustration to help the reader understand the subject.

These paragraphs are easy to recognize and identify because of the use of key words and phrases like "For example," "An illustration of this," and "By way of illustration." These and similar phrases tell the reader that an example or illustrative story is coming up.

Surprisingly, half a chapter, lesson, or article may consist of paragraphs of illustration. Unlike lecturers who are face-to-face with their students, authors are confined by the limitations of print. Because they have no way of knowing whether they are getting their ideas across to their readers, they must use more illustrations than they would when speaking. They cannot take chances; they must be sure that everyone will get the point.

The writer, too, cannot be questioned over a misunderstood concept; there is no way to pause and clarify. It must be certain the first time that the student gets it—there are no second chances. For all of these reasons, we can see why much of what we read is illustrative, even in textbooks.

Selective readers are flexible in their approach. This means that while they may pause over paragraphs that define or explain new concepts, they often speed past paragraphs of illustration. After all, if the reader understands the point being illustrated, he or she doesn't need to linger over additional paragraphs illustrating the same point. The reader can move on to the place where something new is being presented.

1. Paragraphs of illustration are used by the author to help the reader understand a(n) _____.

2. For example, if John wanted to write about his father's love for Roy, he might illustrate by telling about how tenderly his father washed the blood from Roy's _____.

3. Authors cannot see their _____; therefore, they cannot tell how effectively their ideas are coming across.

4. Writers must be certain that their concepts are not questioned or _____.

5. If the reader understands the point being made in a paragraph of illustration, he or she can move on to the place where something _____ is being presented.

3 'Tain't So

Langston Hughes

AUTHOR NOTES—
Langston Hughes was born in Joplin, Missouri, in 1902. He grew up in Kansas and Colorado, attended Columbia College in New York, and received a degree from Lincoln University in Pennsylvania.

Hughes was first recognized as an important literary figure in the 1920s, although much of his early work was criticized by black intellectuals for portraying what they thought to be an unattractive view of black life. For most of his career, Hughes avoided anger and violence in his writing, relying instead on the use of humor to convey his message. Hughes's works, which include novels, short stories, poems, plays, and two autobiographies, have been translated into many languages.

In 1967 Hughes died of congestive heart failure in New York City.

VOCABULARY, PART ONE—

All of these terms are in the story you are about to read. Study each term and its meaning. Then answer the questions below.

As you read the story, notice how each term is used. You will have more questions about the terms later.

spry, energetic and physically active

jasmine, shrub with fragrant yellow or white flowers

thereon, on it

platinum, a silver-white precious metal

albeit, even though

placidly, peacefully; quietly

indignantly, in a manner expressing strong displeasure at something unfair or unjust

serenely, calmly; peacefully

gait, a way of walking

infirmities, ailments; illnesses

1. Which term names something that might grow in a garden?

   _____

2. Which term might you use to describe a person who has the energy to go on and on? _____

3. Which term names a substance that might be used in a ring?

   _____

4. Which term could be used in discussing the various diseases and infections a person has? _____

5. Which term describes how you might respond if someone said something insulting to you? _____

A READING PURPOSE —

In this selection a white woman goes to a faith healer. As you read, try to predict what will happen when the two meet.

---

1 Miss Lucy Cannon was a right nice old white woman, so Uncle Joe always stated, except that she really did *not* like colored folks, not even after she come out West to California. She could never get over certain little southern ways she had, and long as she knowed my Uncle Joe, who hauled her ashes for her, she never would call him *Mister*—nor any other colored man *Mister* neither, for that matter not even the minister of the Baptist Church who was a graduate of San Jose State College. Miss Lucy Cannon just wouldn't call colored folks *Mister* nor *Missus*, no matter who they was, neither *in* Alabama nor in California.

2 She was always ailing around, too, sick with first one thing and then another. Delicate, and ever so often she would have a fainting spell, like all good southern white ladies. Looks like the older she got, the more she would be sick and couldn't hardly get around—that is, until she went to a healer and got cured.

3 And that is one of the funniest stories Uncle Joe ever told me, how old Miss Cannon got cured of her heart and hip in just one cure at the healer's.

4 Seems like for three years or more she could scarcely walk—even with a cane—had a terrible bad pain in her right leg from her knee up. And on her left side her heart was always just about to give out. She was in bad shape, that old southern lady, to be as spry as she was, always giving teas and dinners and working her colored help to death.

5 Well, Uncle Joe says, one New Year's Day in Pasadena a friend of hers, a northern lady who was kinda old and retired also and had come out to California to spend her last days, too, and get rid of some parts of her big bank full of money—this old lady told Miss Cannon, "Darling, you just seem to suffer so all the time, and you say you've tried all the doctors and all kinds of baths and medicines. Why don't you try my way of overcoming? Why don't you try faith?"

6 "Faith, honey?" says old Miss Lucy Cannon, sipping her jasmine tea.

7 "Yes, my dear," says the northern white lady. "Faith! I have one of the best faith healers in the world."

8 "Who is he?" asked Miss Lucy Cannon.

9 "She's a woman, dear," said old Miss Northern White Lady. "And she heals by power. She lives in Hollywood."

10 "Give me her address," said Miss Lucy, "and I'll go to see her. How much do her treatments cost?"

11 Miss Lucy warn't so rich as some folks thought she was.

12 "Only ten dollars, dearest," said the other lady. "Ten dollars a treatment. Go, and you'll come away cured."

13 "I have never believed in such things," said Miss Lucy, "nor disbelieved, either. But I will go and see." And before she could learn any more about the healer, some other friends came in and interrupted the conversation.

14 A few days later, however, Miss Lucy took herself all the way from Pasadena to Hollywood, put up for the weekend with a friend of hers, and thought she would go to see the healer, which she did, come Monday morning early.

15 Using her customary cane and hobbling on her left leg, feeling a bit bad around the heart, and suffering terribly in her mind, she managed to walk slowly but with dignity a half-dozen blocks through the sunshine to the rather humble street in which was located the office and home of the healer.

16 In spite of the bright morning air and the good breakfast she had had, Miss Lucy (according to herself) felt pretty bad, racked with pains and crippled to the use of a cane.

17 When she got to the house she was seeking, a large frame dwelling, newly painted, she saw a sign thereon:

18 MISS PAULINE JONES

19 "So that's her name," thought Miss Lucy, "Pauline Jones, Miss Jones."

20 *Ring and Enter* said a little card above the bell. So Miss Lucy entered. But the first thing that set her back a bit was that nobody received her, so she just sat down to await Miss Jones, the healer who had, she heard, an enormous following in Hollywood. In fact, that's why she had come early, so she wouldn't have to wait long. Now, it was only nine o'clock. The office was open—but empty. So Miss Lucy simply waited. Ten minutes passed. Fifteen. Twenty. Finally she became all nervous and fluttery. Heart and limb! Pain, pain, pain! Not even a magazine to read.

21 "Oh, me!" she said impatiently. "What is this? Why, I never!"

22 There was a sign on the wall that read:

23 BELIEVE

24 "I will wait just ten minutes more," said Miss Lucy, glancing at her watch of platinum and pearls.

25 But before the ten minutes were up another woman entered the front door and sat down. To Miss Lucy's horror she was a colored woman! In fact, a big black colored woman!

26 Said Miss Lucy to herself, "I'll never in the world get used to the North. Now here's a great—my friend says great—faith healer treating darkies! Why, down in Alabama a Negro patient wouldn't dare come in here and sit down with white people like this!"

27 But, womanlike (and having still five minutes to wait), Miss Lucy couldn't keep her mouth shut that long. She just had to talk, albeit to a Negro, so she began on her favorite subject—herself.

28 "I certainly feel bad this morning," she said to the colored woman, condescending to open the conversation.

29 "'Tain't so," answered the Negro woman placidly, which sort of took Miss Lucy back a bit. She lifted her chin.

30 "Indeed, it is so," said she indignantly. "My heart is just about to give out. My breath is short."

31 "'Tain't so a-tall," commented the colored woman.

32 "Why!" gasped Miss Lucy. "Such impudence! I tell you *it is so!* I could hardly get down here this morning."

33 "'Tain't so," said the woman calmly.

34 "Besides my heart," went on Miss Lucy, "my right hip pains me so I can hardly sit here."

35 "I say, 'tain't so."

36 "I tell you it *is* so," screamed Miss Lucy. "Where is the healer? I won't sit here and suffer this—this impudence. I can't! It'll kill me! It's outrageous."

37 "'Tain't so," said the large black woman serenely, whereupon Miss Lucy rose. Her pale face flushed a violent red.

38 "Where is the healer?" she cried, looking around the room.

39 "Right here," said the colored woman.

40 "What?" cried Miss Lucy. "You're the—why—you?"

41 "I'm Miss Jones."

42 "Why, I never heard the like," gasped Miss Lucy. "A *colored* woman as famous as you? Why, you must be lying!"

43 "'Tain't so," said the woman calmly.

44 "Well, I shan't stay another minute," cried Miss Lucy.

45 "Ten dollars, then," said the colored woman. "You've had your treatment, anyhow."

46 "Ten dollars! That's entirely too much!"

47 "'Tain't so."

48 Angrily Miss Lucy opened her pocketbook, threw a ten-dollar bill on the table, took a deep breath, and bounced out. She went three blocks up Sunset Boulevard, walking like the wind, conversing with herself.

49 "'Tain't so,'" she muttered. "'Tain't so!' I tell her I'm sick and she says, 'Tain't so!'"

50 On she went at a rapid gait, stepping like a young girl—so mad she had forgotten all about her infirmities, even her heart—when suddenly she cried, "Lord, have mercy, my cane! For the first time in

three years I'm *without* a cane!"

51 Then she realized that her breath was giving her no trouble at all. Neither was her leg. Her temper mellowed. The sunshine was sweet and warm. She felt good.

52 "Colored folks do have some funny kind of supernatural conjuring powers, I reckon," she said, smiling to herself. Im-

> Poor Miss Lucy—her hip was forever giving her grief, her heart forever about to give out. But when she sought treatment, the medicine was worse than the ailment.

mediately her face went grim again. "But the impudence of 'em! Soon's they get up North—calling herself *Miss* Pauline Jones. The idea! Putting on airs and charging me ten dollars for a handful of '*tain't so's*!"

53 In her mind she clearly heard, "'Tain't so!"

Starting Time [   ]

Reading Time [   ]

Finishing Time [   ]

Reading Rate [   ]

COMPREHENSION —

Read the following questions and statements. For each one, put an X in the box before the option that contains the most complete or accurate answer.

1. Miss Lucy Cannon went to see a
   - ☐ a. medical doctor.
   - ☐ b. college professor.
   - ☒ c. faith healer.
   - ☐ d. Protestant minister.

2. Miss Lucy never overcame her
   - ☐ a. femininity.
   - ☐ b. generosity.
   - ☐ c. religion.
   - ☒ d. prejudice.

3. This passage is told as
   - ☒ a. a narrative.
   - ☐ b. an argument.
   - ☐ c. an autobiography.
   - ☐ d. a parable.

4. Miss Jones could cure Lucy Cannon's hip and heart ailments, but she could not cure Miss Cannon's
   - ☐ a. cancer.
   - ☐ b. old age.
   - ☒ c. feelings of racial superiority.
   - ☐ d. habit of giving teas and dinners.

5. Miss Lucy was a little upset when
   - ☐ a. Uncle Joe hauled ashes.
   - ☐ b. she was told to see Miss Jones.
   - ☒ c. no one received her at Miss Jones's.
   - ☐ d. her friend came to visit her.

6. The author implies that the North is to the South as
   - ☐ a. refusal is to hospitality.
   - ☒ b. acceptance is to rejection.
   - ☐ c. outrage is to civility.
   - ☐ d. tolerance is to violence.

7. During the waiting period Miss Lucy was forced to endure, she was probably being
   - ☐ a. abused.
   - ☒ b. observed.
   - ☐ c. humiliated.
   - ☐ d. ridiculed.

8. Uncle Joe's account of Miss Lucy Cannon's adventure is meant to be
   - ☐ a. serious.
   - ☐ b. insulting.
   - ☐ c. racist.
   - ☐ d. humorous.

9. Miss Lucy was
   - ☐ a. a woman who did not believe in God.
   - ☒ b. a person with imaginary ailments.
   - ☒ c. a hypocrite.
   - ☐ d. an organizer.

10. Langston Hughes's treatment of Miss Lucy Cannon is
    - ☒ a. good-natured.
    - ☐ b. abusive.
    - ☐ c. respectful.
    - ☐ d. filled with bitterness.

Comprehension Skills

1. recalling specific facts
2. retaining concepts
3. organizing facts
4. understanding the main idea
5. drawing a conclusion
6. making a judgment
7. making an inference
8. recognizing tone
9. understanding characters
10. appreciating literary forms

VOCABULARY, PART TWO—

Write the term that makes the most sense in each sentence.

spry   ~~jasmine~~
~~placidly~~   gait
~~infirmities~~

1. Sometimes Miss Lucy Cannon's

   _____

   was so unsteady that she could not walk without

   a cane.

2. At other times she was _____

   and energetic.

3. The northern white lady was calm and spoke to her

   friend _placidly_ .

4. She recommended a faith healer who could cure

   Miss Lucy Cannon's _infirmities_ .

5. As they sat drinking _jasmine_

   tea, Miss Lucy Cannon decided to take her friend's

   advice.

serenely   albeit
platinum   indignantly
thereon

6. Miss Lucy Cannon wore an expensive watch made of

   _____ and pearls.

7. She hobbled up to the door and read the sign

   _____ .

8. When she was ignored for 20 minutes, Miss Lucy

   Cannon began to complain _____ .

9. The faith healer never lost her temper; she re-

   sponded _____ to all Miss

   Lucy Cannon's complaints.

10. Miss Lucy Cannon admitted, _____

    unwillingly, that she was satisfied with the faith

    healer's results.

Comprehension Score   [   ]

Vocabulary Score   [   ]

WRITING—

When did you begin to suspect what was going to happen when Miss Lucy Cannon met the faith healer? What clues in the story helped you? Write a few paragraphs telling when and how you figured things out.

STUDY SKILLS—

Read the following passage and answer the questions that follow it.

Paragraphs of Information

The next paragraphs to examine are the ones used by the author to pass along information on the subject. These paragraphs of information contain names, dates, details, explanations, and other factual information.

In a particular chapter or lesson, the reader can expect to find the meat of the matter in paragraphs like these. This is where the author gets down to business and presents the facts. The essential terms have been defined and illustrated, and now the reader is ready for the substance of the lesson.

Students need to recognize paragraphs of information because these contain the instructional material they are responsible for—the data that may appear on tests later.

In presenting information, the author will probably use one of the following methods of development:

1. State an opinion and give reasons. Look for a clue word used to introduce a series of reasons.

2. Pose a problem and offer a solution. Authors use this method frequently because it incorporates questioning as an aid to learning.

3. Draw a conclusion and then present proof. Actually the proof may come first, preceding the conclusion. Check to be sure that the conclusion logically follows from the proof.

4. Present steps in an argument. Expect a list of points here. Look for the introductory signal and circle the points.

5. Make a comparison or draw a contrast. Frequently used in paragraphs of illustration, this method may be used to present information too.

The paragraphs of information are the heart of the lesson. Study them well.

1. In paragraphs of information, the author gets down to business and presents the _____ .

2. In a paragraph of information, the author may state an opinion and give _____ .

3. An author may pose a problem and offer a solution, because this method uses questioning as an aid to

_____ .

4. The reader should expect a list of points if an author presents steps in a(n) _____ .

5. In an article about Langston Hughes's writing, an author might draw a contrast by saying, "Some of his writing was serious, but other pieces, such as "'Tain't So," had a _____ tone."

4

Jazz

Toni Morrison

AUTHOR NOTES—
Toni Morrison was born in Lorain, Ohio, in 1931. She graduated from Howard University and received her master's degree from Cornell University. She has been a senior editor at Random House and on the faculty of, among others, Yale University and Princeton University.

Morrison's novels include *The Bluest Eye*, *Song of Solomon* (winner of a National Book Critics Circle Award), *Sula*, *Tar Baby*, *Beloved* (winner of a Pulitzer Prize), and *Jazz*. She has also written a play and books of essays. In 1993 Morrison was awarded the Nobel Prize for literature, the first African American to receive the award.

Jazz follows *Beloved* as the second in Morrison's trilogy about different kinds of love.

VOCABULARY, PART ONE—

All of these terms are in the story you are about to read. Study each term and its meaning. Then answer the questions below.

As you read the story, notice how each term is used. You will have more questions about the terms later.

whim, a sudden urge or impulse

severance, additional pay given to employees at the time they are fired

dispossessed, thrown out of a house or other property

intricate, complex; puzzling

malleable, able to be formed into various shapes

specter, something causing terror or dread

stupefied, astonished; bewildered

accommodate, to adjust

deception, illusion; hoax

irrelevant, off the point or subject

1. Which term could describe a bracelet made up of many interwoven parts?

   _____

2. Which term might name an act done without any advance thought?

   _____

3. Which term could describe a substance like clay? _____

4. Which term identifies what you might hope to get if you lost your job?

   _____

5. Which term describes how you might feel if you heard you had just won a million dollars? _____

A READING PURPOSE—

This selection describes what it is like for country people to move into a big city. As you read, look for the ways that people change.

■

1 They met in Vesper County, Virginia, under a walnut tree. She had been working in the fields like everybody else, and stayed past picking time to live with a family twenty miles away from her own. They knew people in common; and suspected they had at least one relative in common. They were drawn together because they had been put together, and all they decided for themselves was when and where to meet at night.

2 Violet and Joe left Tyrell, a railway stop through Vesper County, in 1906, and boarded the colored section of the Southern Sky. When the train trembled approaching the water surrounding the City, they thought it was like them: nervous at having gotten there at last, but terrified of what was on the other side. Eager, a little scared, they did not even nap during the fourteen hours of a ride smoother than a rocking cradle. The quick darkness in the carriage cars when they shot through a tunnel made them wonder if maybe there was a wall ahead to crash into or a cliff hanging over nothing. The train shivered with them at the thought but went on and sure enough there was ground up ahead and the trembling became the dancing under their feet. Joe stood up, his fingers clutching the baggage rack above his head. He felt the dancing better that way, and told Violet to do the same.

3 They were hanging there, a young country couple, laughing and tapping back at the tracks, when the attendant came through, pleasant but unsmiling now that he didn't have to smile in this car full of colored people.

4 "Breakfast in the dining car. Breakfast in the dining car. Good morning. Full breakfast in the dining car." He held a carriage blanket over his arm and from underneath it drew a pint bottle of milk, which he placed in the hands of a young woman with a baby asleep across her knees. "Full breakfast."

5 He never got his way, this attendant. He wanted the whole coach to file into the dining car, now that they could. Immediately, now that they were out of Delaware and a long way from Maryland there would be no green-as-poison curtain separating the colored people eating from the rest of the diners. The cooks would not feel obliged to pile extra helpings on the plates headed for the curtain; three lemon slices in the iced tea, two pieces of coconut cake arranged to look like one—to take the sting out of the curtain; homey it up with a little extra on the plate. Now, skirting the City, there were no green curtains; the whole car could be full of colored people and everybody on a first-come first-serve basis. If only they would. If only they would tuck those little boxes and baskets underneath the seat; close those paper bags, for one, put the bacon-stuffed biscuits back into the cloth they were wrapped in, and troop single file through the five cars ahead on into the dining car, where the table linen was at

20

least as white as the sheets they dried on juniper bushes; where the napkins were folded with a crease as stiff as the ones they ironed for Sunday dinner;

> The call of the City was irresistible, and black people from everywhere came when it beckoned.

where the gravy was as smooth as their own, and the biscuits did not take second place to the bacon-stuffed ones they wrapped in cloth. Once in a while it happened. Some well-shod woman with two young girls, a preacherly kind of man with a watch chain and a rolled-brim hat might stand up, adjust their clothes and weave through the coaches toward the tables, foamy white with heavy silvery knives and forks. Presided over and waited upon by a black man who did not have to lace his dignity with a smile.

6 Joe and Violet wouldn't think of it—paying money for a meal they had not missed and that required them to sit still at, or worse, separated by, a table. Not now. Not entering the lip of the City dancing all the way. Her hip bones rubbed his thigh as they stood in the aisle unable to stop smiling. They weren't even there yet and already the City was speaking to them. They were dancing. And like a million others, chests pounding, tracks controlling their feet, they stared out the windows for first sight of the City that danced with them, proving already how much it loved them. Like a million more they could hardly wait to get there and love it back.

7 Some were slow about it and traveled from Georgia to Illinois, to the City, back to Georgia, out to San Diego and finally, shaking their heads, surrendered themselves to the City. Others knew right away that it was for them, this City and no other. They came on a <u>whim</u> because there it was and why not? They came after much planning, many letters written to and from, to make sure and know how and how much and where. They came for a visit and forgot to go back to tall cotton or short. Discharged with or without honor, fired with or without <u>severance</u>, <u>dispossessed</u> with or without notice, they hung around for a while and then could not imagine themselves anywhere else. Others came because a relative or hometown buddy said, Man, you best see this place before you die; or, We got room now, so pack your suitcase and don't bring no high-top shoes.

8 However they came, when or why, the minute the leather of their soles hit the pavement—there was no turning around. Even if the room they rented was smaller than the heifer's stall and darker than a morning privy, they stayed to look at their number, hear themselves in an audience, feel themselves moving down the street among hundreds of others who moved the way they did, and who, when they spoke, regardless of the accent, treated language like the same <u>intricate</u>, <u>malleable</u> toy designed for their play. Part of why they loved it was the <u>specter</u> they left behind. The slumped spines of the veterans of the 27th Battalion betrayed by the commander for whom they had fought like lunatics. The eyes of thousands, <u>stupefied</u> with disgust at having been imported by Mr. Armour, Mr. Swift, Mr. Montgomery Ward to break strikes then dismissed for having done so. The broken shoes of two thousand Galveston longshoremen that Mr. Mallory would never pay fifty cents an hour like the white ones. The praying palms, the raspy breathing, the quiet children of the ones who had escaped from Springfield Ohio, Springfield Indiana, Greensburg Indiana, Wilmington Delaware, New Orleans Louisiana, after raving whites had foamed all over the lanes and yards of home.

9 The wave of black people running from want and violence crested in the 1870s; the '80s; the '90s but was a steady stream in 1906 when Joe and Violet joined it. Like the others, they were country people, but how soon country people forget. When they fall in love with a city, it is forever, and it is like forever. As though there never was a time when they didn't love it. The minute they arrive at the train station or get off the ferry and glimpse the wide streets and the wasteful lamps lighting them, they know they are born for it. There, in a city, they are not so much new as themselves: their stronger, riskier selves. And in the beginning when they first arrive, and twenty years later when they and the City have grown up, they love that part of themselves so much they forget what loving other people was like—if they ever knew, that is. I don't mean they hate them, no, just that what they start to love is the way a person is in the City; the way a schoolgirl never pauses at a stoplight but looks up and down the street before stepping off the curb; how men <u>accommodate</u> themselves to tall buildings and wee porches, what a woman looks like moving in a crowd, or how shocking her profile is against the backdrop of the East River. The restfulness in kitchen chores when she knows the lamp oil or the staple is just around the corner and not seven miles away; the amazement of throwing open the window and being hypnotized for hours by people on the street below.

10 Little of that makes for love, but it does pump desire. The woman who churned a man's blood as she leaned all alone on a fence by a country road might not expect even to catch his eye in the City. But if she is clipping quickly down the big-city street in heels, swinging her purse, or sitting on a stoop with a cool beer in her hand, dangling her shoe from the toes of her foot, the man, reacting to her posture, to soft skin on stone, the weight of the building stressing the delicate, dangling shoe, is captured. And he'd think it was the woman he wanted, and not some combination of curved stone, and a swinging, high-heeled shoe moving in and out of sunlight. He would know right away the <u>deception</u>, the trick of shapes and light and movement, but it wouldn't matter at all because the deception was part of it too. Anyway, he could feel his lungs going in and out. There is no air in the City but there is breath, and every morning it races through him like laughing gas brightening his eyes, his talk, and his expectations. In no time at all he forgets little pebbly creeks and apple trees so old they lay their branches along the ground and you have to reach down or stoop to pick the fruit. He forgets a sun that used to slide up like the yolk of a good country ■

egg, thick and red-orange at the bottom of the sky, and he doesn't miss it, doesn't look up to see what happened to it or to stars made <u>irrelevant</u> by the light of thrilling, wasteful street lamps.

11 That kind of fascination, permanent and out of control, seizes children, young girls, men of every description, mothers, brides, and barfly women, and if they have their way and get to the City, they feel more like themselves, more like the people they always believed they were. Nothing can pry them away from that; the City is what they want it to be: thriftless, warm, scary and full of amiable strangers. No wonder they forget pebbly creeks and when they do not forget the sky completely think of it as a tiny piece of information about the time of day or night.

Starting Time ☐

Reading Time ☐

Finishing Time ☐

Reading Rate ☐

COMPREHENSION —

Read the following questions and statements. For each one, put an X in the box before the option that contains the most complete or accurate answer.

1. Joe and Violet went to the City in
   ☐ a. 1870.
   ☐ b. 1880.
   ☐ c. 1896.
   ☐ d. 1906.

2. The people who came to the City were mostly
   ☐ a. poor.
   ☐ b. reckless.
   ☐ c. middle-aged.
   ☐ d. timid.

3. This selection presents events
   ☐ a. in chronological order.
   ☐ b. through a series of impressions.
   ☐ c. in spatial order.
   ☐ d. from the point of view of Violet.

4. A good title for this selection would be
   ☐ a. The Lure of the City.
   ☐ b. Getting Rich Quick.
   ☐ c. Making Your Mark.
   ☐ d. Decisions and Desire.

5. The green curtain was removed at the Delaware border because
   ☐ a. it was time for people to go to the dining car.
   ☐ b. there was no law there requiring segregation.
   ☐ c. there was no law there requiring first- and second-class sections.
   ☐ d. the poison on the cloth had to be removed.

6. People were told not to bring high-top shoes because
   ☐ a. they would make them look like country folk.
   ☐ b. they could buy new shoes in the City.
   ☐ c. the shoes would look too heavy on the City streets.
   ☐ d. the styles in shoes changed every year.

7. The events referred to in Springfield, Ohio, and New Orleans were
   ☐ a. small arguments that got out of control.
   ☐ b. cases of job discrimination.
   ☐ c. riots by blacks against whites.
   ☐ d. riots by whites against blacks.

8. In describing the City, the writer creates a sense of its
   - ☐ a. excitement.
   - ☐ b. danger.
   - ☐ c. crowdedness.
   - ☐ d. size.

9. The women of the City are portrayed as
   - ☐ a. prostitutes.
   - ☐ b. desirable.
   - ☐ c. restful.
   - ☐ d. discriminated against.

10. The phrase "a sun that used to slide up like the yolk of a good country egg" is
    - ☐ a. an exaggeration.
    - ☐ b. a symbol.
    - ☐ c. a literal comparison.
    - ☐ d. an imaginative comparison.

Comprehension Skills

1. recalling specific facts
2. retaining concepts
3. organizing facts
4. understanding the main idea
5. drawing a conclusion
6. making a judgment
7. making an inference
8. recognizing tone
9. understanding characters
10. appreciating literary forms

VOCABULARY, PART TWO —

Write the term that makes the most sense in each sentence.

severance   **dispossessed**
specter   **stupefied**
whim

1. Some people came to the City on a _____, but others came because they had serious problems.

2. If a person was _____, he or she might move to the City to find a new home.

3. Some people were _____ if they suddenly lost their jobs without warning.

4. If a person had received _____, it might be possible to go for a little while without working.

5. The _____ of losing another job stayed in people's minds and haunted them.

intricate   **malleable**
accommodate   **deception**
irrelevant

6. In many ways the City seemed like a(n) _____, an illusion that didn't really exist.

7. It was _____; you could shape it to fit whatever fancy you had.

8. People learned to change their ways and _____ themselves to its tall buildings and busy streets.

9. They grew to love the City so much that it became _____ whether or not they would ever return home.

10. All the parts of the City seemed like a(n) _____ puzzle that had to be fitted together.

Comprehension Score [＿＿＿＿＿]

Vocabulary Score [＿＿＿＿＿]

WRITING —

Assume that you are a person from the country going into the City for the first time. Describe your feelings in a few paragraphs. Base your ideas on details you find in the selection.

STUDY SKILLS—

Read the following passage and answer the questions that follow it.

Paragraphs of Definition

You have seen how textbook authors use their paragraphs of introduction to "kick off" the article or chapter. The next paragraph to examine is the one used to define or explain an idea or concept that is unfamiliar to the reader.

Fortunately, these paragraphs of definition are easily recognizable. Frequently, the word, phrase, or concept being defined is shown in italics—this tells the reader that the word or words in italics are being studied and analyzed. Certain key words appear regularly in these paragraphs, words authors use when defining. Look for phrases like "We can define this as..." or "This simply means..." and similar phrases, many of which include the word *define*.

It is essential that the reader recognize these paragraphs because what is defined is important to know and understand. The reader can be certain that much of what is to follow may hinge on his or her understanding of the new word or concept.

Students should study carefully each word in a definition because every word is loaded with essential information. Definitions are by nature precisely constructed. The words have been carefully selected to convey the exact meaning that the concept demands. The greatest mistake a student can make is to hurry past a definition. Instead, the student should look at the contribution each word makes to the total meaning.

Question the author: "What exactly does this word add to the meaning? How would the definition change if this word were left out?" The wise student always pauses and rereads definitions at least once. No other single paragraph may be so essential to comprehension of the chapter.

1. Paragraphs of definition are easily

   _____.

2. Words being studied or analyzed are frequently

   shown in _____.

3. Authors use certain _____

   words when they are defining things.

4. Students should carefully study each word of the definition, because every word is a source of essential

   _____.

5. In this selection, Toni Morrison defines *deception* as "the trick of shapes and light and movement"; in a textbook her definition would be more

   _____ constructed.

5 | Up from Slavery

Booker T. Washington

AUTHOR NOTES—
Booker T. Washington was the most influential black leader and educator of his time in the United States. Born a slave in 1856, he was freed by the United States government in 1865, and later attended the Hampton Institute, an industrial school for blacks and Native Americans in Virginia. Washington became a teacher at Hampton in 1879 and in 1881 founded the Tuskegee Institute, a vocational school for blacks in Alabama.

Washington believed that blacks could benefit more from a practical, vocational education than from a college education. He felt that if black people worked hard, acquired property, and developed a strong economic foundation, they would be granted civil and political rights. In keeping with his moderate stance, Washington never publicly supported black political causes. He did, however, secretly finance lawsuits opposing segregation.

Washington's immensely popular autobiography, *Up From Slavery*, was published in 1901. He remained a powerful leader until his death in 1915.

VOCABULARY, PART ONE—
All of these terms are in the story you are about to read. Study each term and its meaning. Then answer the questions below.

As you read the story, notice how each term is used. You will have more questions about the terms later.

pretentious, making claims to excellence or importance

grave, serious; of some importance

consumed, used up

satchel, a small handbag or suitcase

vessel, a ship

surplus, extra quantity left over

revelation, a new finding or disclosure

indispensable, absolutely necessary

defray, to pay for

prevailing, happening most often; dominant

1. Which term might be used in referring to a boat? _____

2. Which term would you use to describe the extra food left from a party?

    _____

3. Which term describes what happened to the food from the party that was eaten?

    _____

4. Which term could describe winds that always come from the west?

    _____

5. How would you describe a piece of equipment that you could not get along with-

    out? _____

A READING PURPOSE —

This selection discusses Washington's earliest schooling. As you read, decide what is
Washington's strongest quality as he pursues his education.

■

1   One day, while at work in the coal-mine, I happened to overhear two miners talking about a great school for coloured people somewhere in Virginia. This was the first time that I had ever heard anything about any kind of school or college that was more <u>pretentious</u> than the little coloured school in our town.

2   In the darkness of the mine I noiselessly crept as close as I could to the two men who were talking. I heard one tell the other that not only was the school established for the members of my race, but that opportunities were provided by which poor but worthy students could work out all or a part of the cost of board, and at the same time be taught some trade or industry.

3   As they went on describing the school, it seemed to me that it must be the greatest place on earth, and not even Heaven presented more attractions for me at that time than did the Hampton Normal and Agricultural Institute in Virginia, about which those men were talking. I resolved at once to go to that school, although I had no idea where it was, or how many miles away, or how I was going to reach it; I remembered only that I was on fire constantly with one ambition, and that was to go to Hampton. This thought was with me day and night....

4   In the fall of 1872 I determined to make an effort to get there, although, as I have stated, I had no definite idea of the direction in which Hampton was, or of what it would cost to go there. I do not think that any one thoroughly sympathized with me in my ambition to go to Hampton unless it was my mother, and she was troubled with a <u>grave</u> fear that I was starting out on a "wild-goose chase." At any rate, I got only a half-hearted consent from her that I might start. The small amount of money that I had earned had been <u>consumed</u> by my stepfather and the remainder of the family, with the exception of a very few dollars, and so I had very little with which to buy clothes and pay my travelling expenses. My brother John helped me all that he could, but of course that was not a great deal, for his work was in the coal-mine, where he did not earn much, and most of what he did earn went in the direction of paying the household expenses.

5   Perhaps the thing that touched and pleased me most in connection with my starting for Hampton was the interest that many of the older coloured people took in the matter. They had spent the best days of their lives in slavery, and hardly expected to live to see the time when they would see a member of their race leave home to attend a boarding-school. Some of these older people would give me a nickel, others a quarter, or a handkerchief.

6   Finally the great day came, and I started for Hampton. I had only a small, cheap <u>satchel</u> that contained what few articles of clothing I could get. My mother at the time was rather weak and broken in health. I hardly expected to see her again, and thus our parting was all the more sad. She, however, was very brave through it all. At that time there were no through trains connecting that part of West Virginia with eastern Virginia. Trains ran only a portion of the way, and the remainder of the distance was travelled by stage-coaches.

7 The distance from Malden to Hampton is about five hundred miles. I had not been away from home many hours before it began to grow painfully evident that I did not have enough money to pay my fare to Hampton....

> Young Booker T. Washington resolved to go to the Hampton Institute even before he knew where it was. When he found out the school was 500 miles away, he set off anyway...on foot.

8 By walking, begging rides both in wagons and in the cars, in some way, after a number of days, I reached the city of Richmond, Virginia, about eighty-two miles from Hampton. When I reached there, tired, hungry, and dirty, it was late in the night. I had never been in a large city, and this rather added to my misery.... I was completely out of money....

9 I must have walked the streets till after midnight. At last I became so exhausted that I could walk no longer. I was tired. I was hungry, I was everything but discouraged. Just about the time when I reached extreme physical exhaustion, I came upon a portion of a street where the board sidewalk was considerably elevated. I waited for a few minutes, till I was sure that no passers-by could see me, and then crept under the sidewalk and lay for the night upon the ground, with my satchel of clothing for a pillow. Nearly all night I could hear the tramp of feet over my head. The next morning I found myself somewhat refreshed, but was extremely hungry, because it had been a long time since I had had sufficient food. As soon as it became light enough for me to see my surroundings, I noticed that I was near a large ship, and that this ship seemed to be unloading a cargo of pig iron. I went at once to the vessel and asked the captain to permit me to help unload the vessel in order to get money for food. The captain, a white man, who seemed to be kind-hearted, consented. I worked long enough to earn money for my breakfast, and it seems to me, as I remember it now, to have been about the best breakfast that I have ever eaten.

10 My work pleased the captain so well that he told me if I desired I could continue working for a small amount per day. This I was very glad to do. I continued working on this vessel for a number of days. After buying food with the small wages I received there was not much left to add to the amount I must get to pay my way to Hampton. In order to economize in every way possible, so as to be sure to reach Hampton in a reasonable time, I continued to sleep under the same sidewalk that gave me shelter the first night I was in Richmond....

11 When I had saved what I considered enough money with which to reach Hampton, I thanked the captain of the vessel for his kindness, and started again. Without any unusual occurrence I reached Hampton, with a surplus of exactly fifty cents with which to begin my education. To me it had been a long, eventful journey; but the first sight of the large, three-story, brick school building seemed to have rewarded me for all that I had undergone in order to reach the place.... It seemed to me to be the largest and most beautiful building I had ever seen. The sight of it seemed to give me new life. I felt that a new kind of existence had now begun—that life would now have a new meaning. I felt that I had reached the promised land, and I resolved to let no obstacle prevent me from putting forth the highest effort to fit myself to accomplish the most good in the world....

12 Life at Hampton was a constant revelation to me; was constantly taking me into a new world. The matter of having meals at regular hours, of eating on a tablecloth, using a napkin, the use of the bathtub and of the toothbrush, as well as the use of sheets upon the bed, were all new to me....

13 The charge for my board at Hampton was ten dollars per month. I was expected to pay a part of this in cash and to work out the remainder. To meet this cash payment, as I have stated, I had just fifty cents when I reached the institution. Aside from a very few dollars that my brother John was able to send me once in a while, I had no money with which to pay my board. I was determined from the first to make my work as janitor so valuable that my services would be indispensable. This I succeeded in doing to such an extent that I was soon informed that I would be allowed the full cost of my board in return for my work. The cost of tuition was seventy dollars a year. This, of course, was wholly beyond my ability to provide. If I had been compelled to pay the seventy dollars for tuition, in addition to providing for my board, I would have been compelled to leave the Hampton school. General Armstrong, however, very kindly got Mr. S. Griffitts Morgan, of New Bedford, Mass., to defray the cost of my tuition during the whole time that I was at Hampton....

14 After having been for a while at Hampton, I found myself in difficulty because I did not have books

and clothing. Usually, however, I got around the trouble about books by borrowing from those who were more fortunate than myself. As to clothes, when I reached Hampton I had practically nothing. Everything that I possessed was in the small hand satchel....

15 In some way I managed to get on till the teachers learned that I was in earnest and meant to succeed, and then some of them were kind enough to see that I was partly supplied with second-hand clothing that had been sent in barrels from the North. These barrels proved a blessing to hundreds of poor but deserving students. Without them I question whether I should ever have gotten through Hampton....

16 I was among the youngest of the students who were in Hampton at that time. Most of the students were men and women—some as old as forty years of age. As I now recall the scene of my first year, I do not believe that one often has the opportunity of coming into contact with three or four hundred men and women who were so tremendously in earnest as these men and women were. Every hour was occupied in study or work. Nearly all had had enough actual contact with the world to teach them the need of education. Many of the older ones were, of course, too old to master the textbooks very thoroughly, and it was often sad to watch their struggles; but they made up in earnestness much of what ■

they lacked in books. Many of them were as poor as I was, and, besides having to wrestle with their books, they had to struggle with a poverty which prevented their having the necessities of life. Many of them had aged parents who were dependent upon them, and some of them were men who had wives whose support in some way they had to provide for.

17 The great and prevailing idea that seemed to take possession of every one was to prepare himself to lift up the people at his home. No one seemed to think of himself. And the officers and teachers, what a rare set of human beings they were! They worked for the students night and day, in season and out of season. They seemed happy only when they were helping students in some manner. Whenever it is written—and I hope it will be—the part that the Yankee teachers played in the education of the Negroes immediately after the war will make one of the most thrilling parts of the history of this country.

Starting Time	
Reading Time	
Finishing Time	
Reading Rate	

COMPREHENSION —

Read the following questions and statements. For each one, put an X in the box before the option that contains the most complete or accurate answer.

1. Booker T. Washington was raised in
   - ☒ a. Malden, West Virginia.
   - ☐ b. Richmond, Virginia.
   - ☐ c. Hampton, Virginia.
   - ☐ d. Roanoke, Virginia.

2. The teachers at Hampton were
   - ☒ a. sensitive to the needs of the students.
   - ☐ b. impressed with black intellectuals.
   - ☐ c. in tune with the ideas of the community.
   - ☐ d. concerned with economic gain.

3. The events in this selection are presented in
   - ☐ a. order of importance.
   - ☐ b. numerical order.
   - ☐ c. spatial order.
   - ☒ d. chronological order.

4. Which of the following best expresses the theme of the selection?
   - ☒ a. Slow and steady wins the race.
   - ☐ b. A stitch in time saves nine.
   - ☐ c. The truth shall set men free.
   - ☐ d. Virtue is its own reward.

5. Which of the following seems to be true?
   - ☐ a. Hampton was a short distance from Malden.
   - ☒ b. Washington's family was poor.
   - ☐ c. Mr. Morgan was Washington's uncle.
   - ☐ d. General Armstrong disliked Washington.

6. The Yankee teachers at Hampton
   - ☐ a. refused to teach black children.
   - ☒ b. were not prejudiced toward blacks.
   - ☐ c. made better teachers than southern teachers did.
   - ☐ d. were better educated than most teachers.

28

7. There is evidence to suggest that the Hampton Normal and Agricultural Institute received support from
   ☐ a. the federal government.
   ☐ b. black organizations.
   ☐ c. the state of Virginia.
   ☒ d. Northern whites.

8. The tone of the selection is meant to be
   ☐ a. depressing.
   ☐ b. bitter.
   ☐ c. factual.
   ☒ d. inspiring.

9. The selection suggests that Washington was
   ☐ a. remarkable, despite average ability.
   ☐ b. poor, hungry, and lonely.
   ☒ c. ingenious, talented, and industrious.
   ☐ d. insensitive to his family's needs.

10. The selection can best be classified as being
    ☐ a. fictional.
    ☐ b. biographical.
    ☒ c. autobiographical.
    ☐ d. descriptive.

Comprehension Skills

1. recalling specific facts
2. retaining concepts
3. organizing facts
4. understanding the main idea
5. drawing a conclusion
6. making a judgment
7. making an inference
8. recognizing tone
9. understanding characters
10. appreciating literary forms

VOCABULARY, PART TWO—

Write the term that makes the most sense in each sentence.

grave   satchel
vessel   surplus
defray

1. To Washington it was of _____ importance to go to a good school.

2. To _____ the cost of his education, he worked as a janitor.

3. He generally had to spend all his money on food and rarely had a _____.

4. When he first got to Hampton, he saw a _____ docked in the harbor and got a job unloading it.

5. He carried his belongings in a _____, which he sometimes had to use for a pillow.

revelation   consumed
indispensable   pretentious
prevailing

6. Washington thought that a good education was _____ and that he could not succeed without one.

7. The school at Hampton was grander and more _____ than the one in Washington's hometown.

8. The _____ attitude among the students was to help those at home; they thought of little else.

9. Washington realized that this idea of helping others _____ most of his classmates' energy.

10. Because he had had indifferent teachers in the past, it was a _____ to him how much the instructors at Hampton cared about the students.

Comprehension Score [   ]

Vocabulary Score [   ]

WRITING —

What do you think is Washington's strongest quality? Write a few paragraphs giving your opinion. Quote specific passages from the selection to support your opinion.

STUDY SKILLS —

Read the following passage and answer the questions that follow it.

Paragraphs of Transition

The recognizable feature of paragraphs of transition is their brevity—they are normally short.

As the name implies, these paragraphs are used by the author to pass logically from one aspect of the subject to another. Through paragraphs of transition, authors show a change of thought or introduce a new side to the matter under discussion.

Readers should be alert to an upcoming change when they see paragraphs of transition. They should know the author is about to switch tracks and change to a new topic. This knowledge helps the student to organize the reading, because it is obvious that the current discussion is ending and that something new is coming.

Transitional paragraphs are valuable in other ways too. Because they introduce something new, they may function as paragraphs of introduction—they may offer a brief preview of the new concepts the author now plans to discuss; they may state the purpose the author hopes to accomplish by presenting the following information; or they may try to arouse the reader's interest in what is to follow.

In another way, paragraphs of transition may function as a concluding paragraph, summing up for the reader the important points of the aspect being concluded. Or a restatement of the central thought may be presented to help the reader understand the subject before moving on.

It is this combination of functions and its contribution to the reader's understanding of a text's organization that makes the brief paragraph of transition so valuable.

1. Paragraphs of transition are normally

   _____.

2. The reader knows that the current discussion is coming to a(n) _____ when he sees a paragraph of transition.

3. Paragraphs of transition sometimes function as paragraphs of _____ when they state new concepts the author plans to discuss.

4. These paragraphs may be used as _____ paragraphs when they restate a central thought before moving on.

5. In the Washington selection, the paragraph beginning "After having been for a while at Hampton" is a transition paragraph that also serves as a paragraph of _____.

6

Die Nigger Die!

H. Rap Brown

AUTHOR NOTES—
American political activist and author
H. Rap Brown was a controversial civil
rights figure during the 1960s and early
1970s.

Born in Baton Rouge, Louisiana, in
1943, Brown was raised in an orphan-
age by white missionaries. At age 15 he
entered Southern University and became active in the civil rights movement. Brown was the most
revolutionary of the leaders of the Student Nonviolent Coordinating Committee, and he replaced Stokely Carmichael
as chairman in 1967. He also served as
minister of justice for the Black Pan-
thers organization, often giving
speeches advocating black militancy
and rebellious confrontations.

By 1980 Brown had converted to the
Muslim religion and changed his name
to Jamil Abdullah Al'Amin. Currently
this former Black Panther is the propri-
etor of The Community Store in Atlanta,
Georgia.

Die Nigger Die! was published in
1969.

VOCABULARY, PART ONE—
All of these terms are in the story you are about to read.
Study each term and its meaning. Then answer the ques-
tions below.

As you read the story, notice how each term is used.
You will have more questions about the terms later.

conspiracy, a plan made with other people to do something unlawful

inciting, arousing to action

consciousness, awareness of what is in one's own mind

pinnacle, the peak; the highest aspiration

inhumanity, lack of feeling or human qualities

anarchy, disorder and lawlessness

Reich, Nazi state

genocide, killing off of an entire people

due process, legal measures that preserve a person's rights

dissolution, dissolving

31

1. Which term would you use to name a scene where people are running wild in the streets? _____

2. Which term identifies a situation where a group of people are plotting to overthrow a government? _____

3. Which term could describe where a man is if he has just become president of his company? _____

4. What is a term for the attitude of a woman who ignores a wounded person crying out for help? _____

5. Which term describes the systematic murder of the Tutsi people in Africa?

_____

A READING PURPOSE —

In this selection Brown expresses his views of black people's situation in the 1960s.
As you read, decide how much of what he describes is still true.

■

1 While I was in jail in Alexandria, I wrote what was to become a series of Letters from Jail. I didn't plan it like that but that's how it's been working out. I feel when I'm in jail that the people should understand very clearly that the reason I'm in jail is because my crime is political, because I've spoken out against injustices. When I was arrested after Cambridge, the press tried to portray me as some kind of dangerous outlaw. So in my Letters from Jail, I raised the question: Who Are the Real Outlaws?

Brothers and Sisters,

2 *White people are saying that the uprisings of our people in almost 100 american cities "must be a* <u>conspiracy</u>*."* Where is the real conspiracy? *Black people across this country have known that the real conspiracy in this country is to run us out, keep us down or kill us, if we can't act like the honky wants us to act.*

3 *We're fighting for our survival and for this we are called criminals, outlaws and murderers.* Who are the real criminals? *Who stole us from Africa? Who has been stealing our labor these past 400 years to build this country?* Who are the real murderers? *Why don't they call the police who gun us down in the streets every day, all year 'round...why don't they call them murderers?*

4 *Why don't they call Lyndon Johnson a murderer and an outlaw? He fights an illegal war with our brothers and our sons. He sends them to fight against other people of color who are also fighting for their freedom.*

5 *Who are the real outlaws in this country? They say I am an outlaw. I am charged with* <u>inciting</u> *Black people to "riot." It is against the "law" to riot. But did you or I have any say in passing this law? Do we have much of a say in any of the laws passed in this country? I consider myself neither morally nor legally bound to obey laws that were made by a group of white "lawmakers" who did not let my people be represented in making those laws.*

6 *That government which makes laws that you and I are supposed to obey, without letting us be a part of that government...is an illegal government. The men who pass those laws are outlaws; the police who enforce those laws are outlaws and murderers.*

7 *It should be understandable that we, as Black people, should adopt the attitude that we are neither morally nor legally bound to obey laws which were not made with our consent and which seek to keep us "in our place." Nor can we be expected to have confidence in the white man's courts which interpret and enforce those laws. The white man makes all the laws, he drags us before his courts, he accuses us, and he sits in judgment over us.*

8 *White america should not fool itself into believing that if it comes down harder on us that that will keep us from doing what we believe is right. History has shown that when a*

In this letter from jail, H. Rap Brown rips away the veil obscuring the lies and repression of an "illegal government."

man's <u>consciousness</u> is aroused, when a man really believes what he is doing, threats of jail and death cannot turn that man back. The threat of jail or death will not turn me nor others like me from the path we have taken.

9 *We stand on the eve of a Black revolution. These rebellions are but a dress rehearsal for real revolution. For to men, freedom in their own land is the <u>pinnacle</u> of their ambitions, and nothing can turn men aside who have conviction and a strong sense of freedom.*

10 *More powerful than my fear of what could happen to me in prison is my hatred for what happens to my people in those outside prisons called the Black ghettoes of this country. I hate the practice of race discrimination, and in my hatred I am supported by the fact that the overwhelming majority of mankind hates it equally. There is nothing any court can do to me that will change that hatred in me; it can only be changed by the removal of the racism and <u>inhumanity</u> which exists in this country.*

11 *A society which can mount a huge military action against a Black youth who breaks a window, and at the same time plead that it is powerless to protect Black youths who are being murdered each year because they seek to make democracy in america a reality, is a sick, criminal and insane society. They talk about violence in the country's streets! Each time a Black church is bombed or burned, that is violence in our streets! Where are the troops?*

12 *Each time a Black body is found in the swamps of Mississippi or Alabama, that is violence in our land! Where are those murderers?*

13 *Each time Black human rights workers are refused protection by the government, that is <u>anarchy!</u>*

14 *Each time a police officer shoots and kills a Black teenager, that is urban crime! Where is the national leader who will go on t.v. and condemn police crime?*

15 *Black people see america for what it is. It is clear now that white america cannot condemn itself, cannot see the reality of its crimes against mankind. We see america for what it is: the Fourth <u>Reich</u>...and we recognize our course of action.*

16 The repeated attempts that the government has made to silence me represent just one level of <u>genocide</u> that is practiced by america. This genocide can be seen on many different levels. It can be seen actively in Vietnam where 45 percent of the frontline casualties are Black. That's no accident. Another level of genocide can be seen operating in the South, where many Black people live on a starvation level. Over 500 Black people die in Alabama each year for lack of proper food and nourishment. This is happening in a country that sends people to the moon. Yet another level of genocide can be seen in the courts. Any Black man across america who faces a white judge or who faces any court procedure can expect the maximum fine and the maximum sentence. Muhammad Ali, LeRoi Jones, Huey Newton, Ed Oquenda, myself, and thousands of Black men and women across the country have been thrown into prison because we have stood up and challenged the system. Some of the best minds in the Black community are in jail and that's genocide. The most obvious example of genocide is in the concentration camps that america has prepared for Black people. This came about as a result of the McCarran Act of 1950, a law that establishes concentration camps. There is a part, Title II, which suspends the right of <u>due process</u>. That means that there goes the <u>dissolution</u> of all machinery whereby you would be entitled to see a lawyer or go to court. You're arrested and taken off to the camp, without having had an opportunity to state your side of the case. Not that the presentation of your case matters.

17 At the present time, america still lets us use her "legal" machinery and, through legal maneuvers, my attorney was able to get me freed. But this was only after the court set ridiculously high bail. This is nothing short of ransom. I anticipate one day, however, that I will be arrested and there will be no legal procedure any lawyer will be able to use to secure my release. In fact, the first question will not be, Let's get Rap out of jail. It'll be, Where is Rap?

Starting Time	
Reading Time	
Finishing Time	
■ Reading Rate	

COMPREHENSION —

Read the following questions and statements. For each one, put an X in the box before the option that contains the most complete or accurate answer.

1. How many black people die in Alabama each year for lack of proper food and nourishment?
   ☐ a. 100
   ☐ b. 200
   ☐ c. 500
   ☐ d. 600

2. In his letter, H. Rap Brown identifies as "outlaws" the members of
   ☐ a. the legislative branch of the government.
   ☐ b. the judiciary branch of the government.
   ☐ c. the executive branch of the government.
   ☐ d. all of the above.

3. The views stated in Brown's letter are
   ☐ a. old-fashioned.
   ☐ b. unrealistic.
   ☐ c. reflective of his era.
   ☐ d. comparisons.

4. Brown makes clear the point that
   ☐ a. whites are helping blacks.
   ☐ b. slavery still exists in America.
   ☐ c. courts are lenient with blacks.
   ☐ d. blacks must fight for equality.

5. Brown suggests that when he was arrested in Cambridge the press
   ☐ a. treated him with respect.
   ☐ b. was not there.
   ☐ c. gave him unfair coverage.
   ☐ d. misquoted him.

6. Brown is threatening that
   ☐ a. fighting and rioting will occur.
   ☐ b. blacks will fight for freedom in the courts.
   ☐ c. blacks will take over the government.
   ☐ d. a new day of black freedom is just around the corner.

7. Writing the word *america* in all lowercase letters seems to be an act of
   ☐ a. carelessness.
   ☐ b. sloppiness.
   ☐ c. defiance.
   ☐ d. treason.

8. The tone of the selection is
   ☐ a. neutral.
   ☐ b. objective.
   ☐ c. restrained.
   ☐ d. militant.

9. Brown's personality can best be described as
   ☐ a. unconcerned.
   ☐ b. aggressive.
   ☐ c. humble.
   ☐ d. complacent.

10. The author's style is
    ☐ a. formal.
    ☐ b. wordy.
    ☐ c. pompous.
    ☐ d. informal.

Comprehension Skills
1. recalling specific facts
2. retaining concepts
3. organizing facts
4. understanding the main idea
5. drawing a conclusion
6. making a judgment
7. making an inference
8. recognizing tone
9. understanding characters
10. appreciating literary forms

VOCABULARY, PART TWO —

Write the term that makes the most sense in each sentence.

conspiracy   inhumanity
Reich   genocide
dissolution

1. Brown sees conditions in the United States as similar to those in the Third _____ in Germany.

2. He feels that _____ has been committed against black people in the same way that Hitler committed it against the Jews.

3. He sees black youth being murdered for expressing their views as an example of the government's _____.

34

4. He believes that the government is involved in a
_____ to keep blacks from
their lawful rights.

5. A _____ of all laws would
mean that those laws would no longer exist.

anarchy   **inciting**
consciousness   **pinnacle**
due process

6. Brown's fiery comments about the government were
seen as _____ black people to
riot.

7. Brown believed that people had to be aware
of injustices against them—that their
_____ had to be raised.

8. He knew that if _____ were
suspended, measures that protected people rights
would no longer exist.

9. A person like Brown might be in the deepest depths
of imprisonment and yet still be at the
_____ of his influence.

10. He would not have been surprised if blacks resorted
to total lawlessness and _____.

Comprehension Score [   ]

Vocabulary Score [   ]

W R I T I N G —

How much have conditions in the United States changed
since Brown wrote this letter? Write a short essay
expressing your views. In your essay, mention specific
points from Brown's letter and compare them to the way
things are today.

S T U D Y   S K I L L S —

Read the following passage and answer the questions
that follow it.

Closing Paragraphs

We have been discussing the different ways that authors
use paragraphs in presenting their subject and how the
wise reader profits from recognizing these functions.

The function of the closing paragraph is to give the
reader the author's concluding remarks or final words on
the subject. The author may do this in one of several
ways.

First, although rarely done, the author may draw a
conclusion based on the information contained in the
lesson or chapter. Authors are reluctant to proceed in
this way because conclusions based on an entire chapter
are much too important to be mentioned just once, at
the end. We can expect to find the conclusion given early
in the chapter and the facts supporting it to follow. It is
likely, though, that such an important conclusion would
be repeated or restated in the final paragraph.

Second, the author may use the final paragraph to
summarize. Here, for the last time, is the opportunity to
give the reader points made during the presentation. In
effect, the author is saying, "Above all, remember this.
This is what it's all been about." These summarizing remarks are valuable to the learner and become a definite
aid in reviewing.

Last, the author may choose to leave the readers with
one final thought—the central, all-inclusive idea around
which the chapter was developed. Occasionally this will
be done with an anecdote, story, or moral used as a cap
to the discussion.

The concluding paragraph is the author's last chance
to reach the audience. If he or she wants to leave the
readers with a last thought, here is where it will be.

1. The paragraphs used by the author to finish his remarks on a subject are called _____
paragraphs.

2. The reader can usually expect the conclusion to be
given early in the chapter and the
_____ supporting it to follow.

35

3. Summarizing remarks are a definite aid in

    _____.

4. The author will sometimes include an anecdote,

    story, or _____ to complete the

    discussion.

5. If H. Rap Brown had decided to close with an

    anecdote, he probably would have used one

    describing his unjust treatment by the United States

    _____.

7

What to the Slave Is the 4th of July?

Frederick Douglass

AUTHOR NOTES—

Born a slave in Maryland in 1817, Frederick Douglass escaped from bondage in 1838 and became a leading figure in the antislavery movement. He gained fame as an antislavery orator and told his life story in three autobiographies, which he wrote at three different stages of his life.

After his first autobiography was published in 1845, Douglass traveled to England where he continued to speak against slavery. There he made friends who purchased his freedom legally in 1846. Upon returning to the United States in 1847, Douglass founded the antislavery newspaper, the *North Star*, in Rochester, New York. He also discussed the problems of slavery with President Abraham Lincoln several times and served as United States minister to Haiti from 1889 to 1891. Douglass died in 1895.

VOCABULARY, PART ONE—

All of these terms are in the story you are about to read. Study each term and its meaning. Then answer the questions below.

As you read the story, notice how each term is used. You will have more questions about the terms later.

embodied, put into a definite form or into one place

irony, an occurrence that is the opposite of what is expected

tumultuous, noisy; agitated

jubilant, elated; overjoyed

fettered, bound; restrained

denounce, to express strong disapproval; to condemn publicly

rebuke, to scold

enactments, laws; decrees

discourse, talk; discussion

flay, to beat; to whip

1. Which term describes the condition of prisoners who are in chains?

    _____

2. Which term describes the action of a woman in a public meeting who loudly criticizes someone who disagrees with her? _____

3. Which term could name a situation when there is no rain all day—except when you have scheduled an outdoor activity? _____

4. Which term describes the action of a parent who sternly tells the children that they are misbehaving? _____

5. Which term might be used as a synonym for *conversation*?

    _____

A READING PURPOSE—

This selection discusses the contrast between Fourth of July celebrations and the fact of slavery. As you read, notice the specifics Frederick Douglass uses to emphasize that contrast.

■

1 Fellow citizens, pardon me, and allow me to ask, why am I called upon to speak here today? What have I or those I represent to do with your national independence? Are the great principles of political freedom and of natural justice, <u>embodied</u> in that Declaration of Independence, extended to us? And am I, therefore, called upon to bring our humble offering to the national altar, and to confess the benefits, and express devout gratitude for the blessings resulting from your independence to us?

2 Would to God, both for your sakes and ours, that an affirmative answer could be truthfully returned to these questions. Then would my task be light, and my burden easy and delightful. For who is there so cold that a nation's sympathy could not warm him? Who so obdurate and dead to the claims of gratitude, that would not thankfully acknowledge such priceless benefits? Who so stolid and selfish that would not give his voice to swell the hallelujahs of a nation's jubilee, when the chains of servitude had been torn from his limbs? I am not that man....

3 I am not included within the pale of this glorious anniversary! Your high independence only reveals the immeasurable distance between us. The blessings in which you this day rejoice are not enjoyed in common. The rich inheritance of justice, liberty, prosperity, and independence bequeathed by your fathers is shared by you, not by me. The sunlight that brought life and healing to you has brought stripes and death to me. This Fourth of July is *yours*, not *mine*. *You* may rejoice, *I* must mourn. To drag a man in fetters into the grand illuminated temple of liberty, and call upon him to join you in joyous anthems, were inhuman mockery and sacrilegious <u>irony</u>. Do you mean, citizens, to mock me, by asking me to speak today?...

4 Fellow citizens, above your national, <u>tumultuous</u> joy, I hear the mournful wail of millions! whose chains, heavy and grievous yesterday, are to-day, rendered more intolerable by the <u>jubilant</u> shouts that reach them. If I do forget, if I do not remember those bleeding children of sorrow this day, "may my right hand forget her cunning, and may my tongue cleave to the roof of my mouth!" To forget them, to pass lightly over their wrongs, and to chime in with the popular theme, would be treason most scandalous and shocking, and would make me a reproach before God and the world. My subject, then, fellow citizens, is American slavery. I shall see this day and its popular characteristics from the slave's point of view. Standing here, identified with the American bondman, making his wrongs mine, I do not hesitate to declare, with all my soul, that the character and conduct of this nation never looked blacker to me than on this 4th of July. Whether we turn to the declarations of the past, or to the

professions of the present, the conduct of the nation seems equally hideous and revolting. America is false to the past, false to the present, and solemnly binds herself to be false to the future. Standing with God and the crushed and bleeding slave on this occasion, I will, in the name of humanity, which is outraged, in the name of liberty, which is fettered, in the name of the constitution and the Bible which are disregarded and trampled upon, dare to call in question and to denounce, with all the emphasis I can command, everything that serves to perpetuate slavery—the great sin and shame of America! "I will not equivocate; I will not excuse"; I will use the severest language I can command; and yet not one word shall escape me that any man, whose judgment is not blinded by prejudice, or who is not at heart a slaveholder, shall not confess to be right and just.

This excerpt is from an address that Frederick Douglass, a powerful orator, delivered in Rochester, New York, on July 5, 1852.

5 But I fancy I hear some of my audience say, "It is just in this circumstance that you and your brother abolitionists fail to make a favorable impression on the public mind. Would you argue more and denounce less; would you persuade more and rebuke less; your cause would be much more likely to succeed." But, I submit, where all is plain there is nothing to be argued. What point in the anti-slavery creed would you have me argue? On what branch of the subject do the people of this country need light? Must I undertake to prove that the slave is a man? That point is conceded already. Nobody doubts it. The slaveholders themselves acknowledge it in the enactment of laws for their government. They acknowledge it when they punish disobedience on the part of the slave. There are seventy-two crimes in the State of Virginia, which, if committed by a black man (no matter how ignorant he be), subject him to the punishment of death; while only two of the same crimes will subject a white man to like punishment. What is this but the acknowledgment that the slave is a moral, intellectual, and responsible being? The manhood of the slave is conceded. It is admitted in the fact that Southern statute-books are covered with enactments, forbidding, under severe fines and penalties, the teaching of the slave to read and write. When you can point to any such laws in reference to the beasts of the field, then I may consent to argue the manhood of the slave. When the dogs in your streets, when the fowls of the air, when the cattle on your hills, when the fish of the sea, and the reptiles that crawl, shall be unable to distinguish the slave from a brute, then I will argue with you that the slave is a man!

6 For the present it is enough to affirm the equal manhood of the Negro race. It is not astonishing that, while we are plowing, planting, and reaping, using all kinds of mechanical tools, erecting houses, constructing bridges, building ships, working in metals of brass, iron, copper, silver, and gold; that while we are reading, writing, and cyphering, acting as clerks, merchants and secretaries, having among us lawyers, doctors, ministers, poets, authors, editors, orators, and teachers; that while we are engaged in all the enterprises common to other men—digging gold in California, capturing the whale in the Pacific, feeding sheep and cattle on the hillside, living, moving, acting, thinking, planning, living in families as husbands, wives, and children, and above all, confessing and worshipping the Christian's God, and looking hopefully for life and immortality beyond the grave, we are called upon to prove that we are men?

7 Would you have me argue that man is entitled to liberty? That he is the rightful owner of his own body? You have already declared it. Must I argue the wrongfulness of slavery? Is that a question for Republicans? Is it to be settled by the rules of logic and argumentation, as a matter beset with great difficulty, involving a doubtful application of the principle of justice, hard to be understood? How should I look to-day, in the presence of Americans, dividing and subdividing a discourse, to show that men have a natural right to freedom, speaking of it relatively and positively, negatively and affirmatively? To do so, would be to make myself ridiculous, and to offer an insult to your understanding. There is not a man beneath the canopy of heaven who does not know that slavery is wrong *for him*.

8 What, am I to argue that it is wrong to make men brutes, to rob them of their liberty, to work them without wages, to keep them ignorant of their relations to their fellow men, to beat them with sticks, to flay their flesh with the lash, to load their limbs with irons, to hunt them with dogs, to sell them at auction, to sunder their families, to knock out their teeth, to burn their flesh, to starve them into obedience and submission to their masters? Must I argue that a system thus marked with blood, and stained with pollution, is wrong? No! I will not.

I have better employment for my time and strength than such arguments would imply.

9 What, then, remains to be argued? Is it that slavery is not divine; that God did not establish it; that our doctors of divinity are mistaken? There is blasphemy in the thought. That which is inhuman cannot be divine. Who can reason on such a proposition? They that can, may; I cannot. The time for such argument is passed.

10 At a time like this, scorching irony, not convincing argument, is needed. O! had I the ability, and could I reach the nation's ear, I would, to-day, pour out a fiery stream of biting ridicule, blasting reproach, withering sarcasm, and stern rebuke. For it is not light that is needed, but fire; it is not the gentle shower, but thunder. We need the storm, the whirlwind, and the earthquake. The feeling of the nation must be quickened; the conscience of the nation must be exposed; and its crimes against God and man must be denounced.

11 What, to the American slave, is your 4th of July? I answer, a day that reveals to him more than all other days of the year, the gross injustice and cruelty to which he is the constant victim. To him, your celebration is a sham; your boasted liberty an unholy license; your national greatness, swelling vanity; your sounds of rejoicing are empty and ■ heartless; your denunciation of tyrants, brassfronted impudence; your shouts of liberty and equality, hollow mockery; your prayers and hymns, your sermons and thanksgivings, with all your religious parade and solemnity, are to Him, mere bombast, fraud, deception, impiety, and hypocrisy—a thin veil to cover up crimes which would disgrace a nation of savages. There is not a nation of the earth guilty of practices more shocking and bloody than are the people of these United States, at this very hour.

12 Go where you may, search where you will, roam through all the monarchies and despotisms of the Old World, travel through South America, search out every abuse and when you have found the last, lay your facts by the side of the everyday practices of this nation, and you will say with me that, for revolting barbarity and shameless hypocrisy, America reigns without a rival.

Starting Time	
Reading Time	
Finishing Time	
Reading Rate	

COMPREHENSION —

Read the following questions and statements. For each one, put an X in the box before the option that contains the most complete or accurate answer.

1. The topic of Douglass's speech is
   - ☐ a. The Promised Land.
   - ☐ b. God's Great Promise.
   - ☐ c. American Slavery.
   - ☐ d. Freedom Lives.

2. The attitude of the slave owner toward his slaves was contradictory because he
   - ☐ a. held them accountable for their actions.
   - ☐ b. permitted them to hold church meetings.
   - ☐ c. destroyed the unity of the black family.
   - ☐ d. encouraged them to work for their freedom.

3. What type of order is this speech presented in?
   - ☐ a. climactic
   - ☐ b. chronological
   - ☐ c. historical
   - ☐ d. spatial

4. Viewed in the light of Douglass's speech, the Fourth of July celebrations can be considered
   - ☐ a. appropriate.
   - ☐ b. hypocritical.
   - ☐ c. patriotic.
   - ☐ d. artificial.

5. To Frederick Douglass, the gay, noisy Fourth of July celebrations
   - ☐ a. suggested hope for his oppressed race.
   - ☐ b. made him fear a violent slave uprising.
   - ☐ c. filled him with doubt and concern.
   - ☐ d. were cruel reminders of inhuman injustice.

6. When Douglass gave this speech, he expected that
   - ☐ a. the slaves would be freed immediately.
   - ☐ b. a riot would follow.
   - ☐ c. the slaves would not be freed in his lifetime.
   - ☐ d. many would be made uncomfortable by his statements.

7. Generally, the slave owners viewed their slaves in no better light than they did their animals because
   ☐ a. they sought a moral justification for slavery.
   ☐ b. they were morally justified as slave owners.
   ☐ c. the American Constitution denied the slaves their human rights.
   ☐ d. the slaves offered no resistance to their white masters.

8. The tone of the speech is one of
   ☐ a. inquiry.
   ☐ b. militancy.
   ☐ c. humility.
   ☐ d. criticism.

9. We can tell from this speech that Douglass is
   ☐ a. poor and bitter.
   ☐ b. intelligent and angry.
   ☐ c. egotistical and elitist.
   ☐ d. illiterate and humble.

10. Throughout his speech, the author relies heavily on
   ☐ a. questions.
   ☐ b. direct quotations.
   ☐ c. comparisons.
   ☐ d. exaggerations.

Comprehension Skills
1. recalling specific facts
2. retaining concepts
3. organizing facts
4. understanding the main idea
5. drawing a conclusion
6. making a judgment
7. making an inference
8. recognizing tone
9. understanding characters
10. appreciating literary forms

VOCABULARY, PART TWO—
Write the term that makes the most sense in each sentence.

jubilant   **fettered**
denounce   **flay**
irony

1. Douglas saw a great _____ in celebrations of freedom when so many people owned slaves.

2. How could there be celebrations, he wondered, when slaves were _____ in chains?

3. If a slaveholder didn't like what his slaves did, he could _____ them with whips.

4. Instead of feeling _____ , people should really be feeling remorseful.

5. They should _____ slavery for the wicked thing that it is.

enactments   **discourse**
embodied   **tumultuous**
rebuke

6. Douglass was not afraid to _____ his listeners for the things he felt they were doing wrong.

7. To him, celebrations in the face of slavery _____ all that was wrong with American society.

8. He hoped that through public _____ fair-minded people could discuss their opinions with others.

9. The hope was that informed public opinion would lead to new laws and _____ .

10. Then the _____ , cheering crowds would have something worthwhile to celebrate.

Comprehension Score [ ]

Vocabulary Score [ ]

WRITING—
Douglass says that slaveholders know their slaves are human beings. In your own words, write a paragraph that explains his reasoning when he makes this statement.

STUDY SKILLS —

Read the following passage and answer the questions that follow it.

Inflexible Readers

If the reading habits of most of today's adults were to be described, the single adjective *inflexible* would be the most appropriate description.

To understand what is meant by inflexible reading, take the situation that many doctors find themselves in. All of their school years and much of their adult lives have been spent studying vitally important material. Doctors must understand the content of textbooks and journals thoroughly; 100 percent comprehension is required. Accordingly, medical students develop an appropriate reading skill—a thorough, slow, and careful technique leading to mastery of many critical details. The problem comes later, after medical school, when the doctor wants to settle down for an evening's enjoyment with a good novel. Most novels don't require the painstaking attention to detail that a medical text demands. But because of habits formed during years of study, the doctor has become an inflexible reader and plods intensively through whatever kind of reading material that comes to hand.

Medicine isn't the only profession that demands this technique. Lawyers, scientists, and engineers tend to read everything in the specialized way that is used to read professional texts.

As students, we also are guilty of inflexible reading. One factor leading to this is in the way we are first taught to read. Most of us were required to read aloud from our beginning texts. By listening to us, teachers could evaluate our progress and see how well we were learning to recognize, identify, and understand words. Our parents, too, could tell how we were doing by listening to us read.

But, as beginning readers, we often learn other things at the same time: we are taught to read quite slowly and to pronounce words carefully, we are taught not to skip words, and we are conditioned to read in this one acceptable fashion. So, as we learn to read, the habits that will later make us inflexible readers are being established.

1. A word that can be used to describe the reading habits of many adults is _____ .

2. No dedicated doctor is satisfied with less than _____ comprehension.

3. One factor leading to inflexibility can be found in the way students are _____ to read.

4. As beginners, we are _____ to read in one acceptable fashion.

5. Following this fashion, when most students read Frederick Douglass's speech, they read it quite _____ .

8 The Autobiography of Malcolm X

Malcolm X with Alex Haley

AUTHOR NOTES —

Malcolm X was born Malcolm Little in 1925. At age 21, he was imprisoned for burglary. In prison, he adopted the beliefs of the Black Muslims, a religious group that advocated separation of the races. Following his release, he rose through the ranks of the Black Muslims, but broke with them in 1964 because of disagreements with their leader, the prophet Elijah Muhammad. After a trip to Mecca and conversion to orthodox Islam, Malcolm X organized his own Islamic religious center, the Muslim Mosque, Inc. and changed his name to El-Hajj Malik al-Shabazz. He also formed the Organization of Afro-American Unity, which sought political rights for black Americans. In 1965, he was assassinated at a meeting in Harlem.

The Autobiography of Malcolm X was published in 1965. In 1992, the African American filmmaker Spike Lee released his movie, *X*, which spurred new interest in Malcolm X.

VOCABULARY, PART ONE —

All of these terms are in the story you are about to read. Study each term and its meaning. Then answer the questions below.

As you read the story, notice how each term is used. You will have more questions about the terms later.

objectively, fairly; without bias

inevitable, unavoidable

propagating, spreading; disseminating

parasite, a person or thing that lives off another

salving, smoothing over; soothing

malignancy, an evil; a cancer

linguist, a person who has skill with languages

unspeakable, outrageous; terrible

invariably, constantly; unchangingly

demagogue, a leader who stirs people up so they will obey his or her wishes

1. Which term might you use in describing someone who has lived in your apartment for six months without paying any room and board? _____

2. Which term describes how a person acts when she looks at all sides of an issue before making a decision? _____

3. Which term could describe a person who speaks German, Portuguese, and Chinese?

   _____

4. Which term could describe a church leader whose preaching gets his congregation to start rioting? _____

5. If I walk along the river at seven o'clock every single morning, which term could be used in telling how often I am there? _____

A READING PURPOSE—

In this selection Malcolm X reviews events of his life. As you read, look particularly for his views on education.

■

1 I have given to this book so much of whatever time I have because I feel, and I hope, that if I honestly and fully tell my life's account, read objectively it might prove to be a testimony of some social value.

2 I think that an objective reader may see how in the society to which I was exposed as a black youth here in America, for me to wind up in a prison was really just about inevitable. It happens to so many thousands of black youth.

3 I think that an objective reader may see how when I heard "The white man is the devil," when I played back what had been my own experiences, it was inevitable that I would respond positively; then the next twelve years of my life were devoted and dedicated to propagating that phrase among the black people.

4 I think, I hope, that the objective reader, in following my life—the life of only one ghetto-created Negro—may gain a better picture and understanding than he has previously had of the black ghettoes which are shaping the lives and the thinking of almost all of the 22 million Negroes who live in America.

5 Thicker each year in these ghettoes is the kind of teen-ager that I was—with the wrong kinds of heroes, and the wrong kinds of influences. I am not saying that all of them become the kind of parasite that I was. Fortunately, by far most do not. But

still, the small fraction who do add up to an annual total of more and more costly, dangerous youthful criminals. The F.B.I. not long ago released a report of a shocking rise in crime each successive year since the end of World War II—ten to twelve percent each year. The report did not say so in so many words, but I am saying that the majority of that crime increase is annually spawned in the black ghettoes which the American racist society permits to exist. In the 1964 "long, hot summer" riots in major cities across the United States, the socially disinherited black ghetto youth were always at the forefront.

6 In this year, 1965, I am certain that more—and worse—riots are going to erupt, in yet more cities, in spite of the conscience-salving Civil Rights Bill. The reason is that the *cause* of these riots, the racist malignancy in America, has been too long unattended.

7 I believe that it would be almost impossible to find anywhere in America a black man who has lived further down in the mud of human society than I have; or a black man who has been any more ignorant than I have been; or a black man who has suffered more anguish during his life than I have. But it is only after the deepest darkness that the greatest light can come; it is only after extreme grief that the greatest joy can come; it is only after

slavery and prison that the sweetest appreciation of freedom can come.

8 For the freedom of my 22 million black brothers and sisters here in America, I do believe that I

In this excerpt from his autobiography, Malcolm X looks back at his life and foretells his own assassination.

have fought the best that I knew how, and the best that I could, with the shortcomings that I have had. I know that my shortcomings are many.

9 My greatest lack has been, I believe, that I don't have the kind of academic education I wish I had been able to get—to have been a lawyer, perhaps. I do believe that I might have made a good lawyer. I have always loved verbal battle, and challenge. You can believe me that if I had the time right now, I would not be one bit ashamed to go back into any New York City public school and start where I left off at the ninth grade, and go on through a degree. Because I don't begin to be academically equipped for so many of the interests that I have. For instance, I love languages. I wish I were an accomplished linguist. I don't know anything more frustrating than to be around people talking something you can't understand. Especially when they are people who look just like you. In Africa, I heard original mother tongues, such as Hausa, and Swahili, being spoken, and there I was standing like some little boy, waiting for someone to tell me what had been said; I never will forget how ignorant I felt.

10 Aside from the basic African dialects, I would try to learn Chinese, because it looks as if Chinese will be the most powerful political language of the future. And already I have begun studying Arabic, which I think is going to be the most powerful spiritual language of the future.

11 I would just like to *study*. I mean ranging study, because I have a wide-open mind. I'm interested in almost any subject you can mention. I know this is the reason I have come to really like, as individuals, some of the hosts of radio or television panel programs I have been on, and to respect their minds—because even if they have been almost steadily in disagreement with me on the race issue, they still have kept their minds open and objective about the truths of things happening in this world. Irv Kupcinet in Chicago, and Barry Farber, Barry Gray and Mike Wallace in New York—people like them. They also let me see that they respected my mind—

in a way I know they never realized. The way I knew was that often they would invite my opinion on subjects off the race issue. Sometimes, after the programs, we would sit around and talk about all kinds of things, current events and other things, for an hour or more. You see, most whites, even when they credit a Negro with some intelligence, will still feel that all he can talk about is the race issue; most whites never feel that Negroes can contribute anything to other areas of thought, and ideas. You just notice how rarely you will ever hear whites asking any Negroes what they think about the problem of world health, or the space race to land men on the moon.

12 Every morning when I wake up, now, I regard it as having another borrowed day. In any city, wherever I go, making speeches, holding meetings of my organization, or attending to other business, black men are watching every move I make, awaiting their chance to kill me. I have said publicly many times that I know that they have their orders. Anyone who chooses not to believe what I am saying doesn't know the Muslims in the Nation of Islam.

13 But I am also blessed with faithful followers who are, I believe, as dedicated to me as I once was to Mr. Elijah Muhammad. Those who would hunt a man need to remember that a jungle also contains those who hunt the hunters.

14 I know, too, that I could suddenly die at the hands of some white racists. Or I could die at the hands of some Negro hired by the white man. Or it could be some brainwashed Negro acting on his own idea that by eliminating me he would be helping out the white man, because I talk about the white man the way I do.

15 Anyway, now, each day I live as if I am already dead, and I tell you what I would like for you to do. When I *am* dead—I say it that way because from the things I *know*, I do not expect to live long enough to read this book in its finished form—I want you to just watch and see if I'm not right in what I say: that the white man, in his press, is going to identify me with "hate."

16 He will make use of me dead, as he has made use of me alive, as a convenient symbol of "hatred"—and that will help him to escape facing the truth that all I have been doing is holding up a mirror to reflect, to show, the history of unspeakable crimes that his race has committed against my race.

17 You watch. I will be labeled as, at best, an "irresponsible" black man. I have always felt about this accusation that the black "leader" whom white men

consider to be "responsible" is <u>invariably</u> the black "leader" who never gets any results. You only get action as a black man if you are regarded by the white man as "irresponsible." In fact, this much I had learned when I was just a little boy. And since I have been some kind of a "leader" of black people here in the racist society of America, I have been more reassured each time the white man resisted me, or attacked me harder—because each time made me more certain that I was on the right track in the American black man's best interests. The racist white man's opposition automatically made me know that I did offer the black man something worthwhile.

18 Yes, I have cherished my "<u>demagogue</u>" role. I know that societies often have killed the people who have ■

helped to change those societies. And if I can die having brought any light, having exposed any meaningful truth that will help to destroy the racist cancer that is malignant in the body of America— then, all of the credit is due to Allah. Only the mistakes have been mine.

Starting Time [ ]

Reading Time [ ]

Finishing Time [ ]

Reading Rate [ ]

COMPREHENSION —

Read the following questions and statements. For each one, put an X in the box before the option that contains the most complete or accurate answer.

1. Which language does the author predict will be the most powerful politically?
   - ☐ a. Russian
   - ☐ b. Chinese
   - ☐ c. English
   - ☐ d. French

2. Which of the following does the author cite as a subtle form of prejudice inflicted upon black guests by television hosts?
   - ☐ a. limiting guest's questions to racial issues
   - ☐ b. excluding black guests from panel discussions
   - ☐ c. diverting attention from racial issues to general subjects
   - ☐ d. minimizing black accusations through humorous interjections

3. The author makes his point clear by
   - ☐ a. listing personal opinions.
   - ☐ b. showing cause and effect.
   - ☐ c. comparing two cultures.
   - ☐ d. introducing a time order.

4. The selection can be considered
   - ☐ a. a justification of Malcolm X's life and convictions.
   - ☐ b. the final document of a man who has fought well but lost.
   - ☐ c. autobiographical and therefore lacking in objectivity.
   - ☐ d. the work of a demagogue.

5. We can conclude from the selection that Malcolm X
   - ☐ a. was born in the South.
   - ☐ b. could never hold a decent job.
   - ☐ c. believed in peaceful change.
   - ☐ d. did not have a high school diploma.

6. Which of the following black leaders used an approach similar to Malcolm X's?
   - ☐ a. Dr. Martin Luther King, Jr.
   - ☐ b. George Washington Carver
   - ☐ c. H. Rap Brown
   - ☐ d. Bill Cosby

7. "Those who would hunt a man need to remember that a jungle also contains those who hunt the hunters." That statement can be considered a
   - ☐ a. promise.
   - ☐ b. surrender.
   - ☐ c. challenge.
   - ☐ d. warning.

8. The tone of this selection is
   - ☐ a. humorous.
   - ☐ b. matter-of-fact.
   - ☐ c. threatening.
   - ☐ d. sarcastic.

9. From the details Malcolm X reveals about his own background, one is impressed by his
   - ☐ a. lack of personal objectivity.
   - ☐ b. lack of foresight in the face of danger.
   - ☐ c. humble, candid, and frank admissions.
   - ☐ d. rise to prominence in spite of his illiteracy.

10. This selection presents
   ☐ a. numerical facts.
   ☐ b. a fictional story.
   ☐ c. puzzling parables.
   ☐ d. biographical data.

Comprehension Skills
1. recalling specific facts
2. retaining concepts
3. organizing facts
4. understanding the main idea
5. drawing a conclusion
6. making a judgment
7. making an inference
8. recognizing tone
9. understanding characters
10. appreciating literary forms

VOCABULARY, PART TWO —
Write the term that makes the most sense in each sentence.

propagating   **parasite**
salving   **linguist**
invariably

1. Malcolm X wanted to be a _____ so that he could understand African languages when he heard them.

2. He did not want to be considered a _____, someone who couldn't support himself.

3. Malcolm X got upset with talk show hosts because every time he spoke with them, they _____ wanted to discuss race relations.

4. Though he did use forums like talk shows for _____ his opinions, he would not have minded conversations on other topics.

5. Perhaps the shows' hosts felt guilty and listened to Malcolm X as a means of _____ their own consciences.

malignancy   **objectively**
inevitable   **demagogue**
unspeakable

6. As Malcolm X got older, he could look at all sides of an issue and think about it _____.

7. He knew that some _____ outrages had been committed against black people.

8. Unless the _____ of discrimination could be cut from society, its poison would continue to grow and spread.

9. Clashes between blacks and whites were not _____; they could be avoided.

10. He didn't mind being called a _____ if he could stir people up to get results.

Comprehension Score ☐

Vocabulary Score ☐

WRITING —
How did Malcolm X expect to be regarded by whites after his death? How do you think he is actually regarded by white society today? Write a few paragraphs discussing both of these questions.

STUDY SKILLS —
Read the following passage and answer the questions that follow it.

Flexible Readers
Good readers are flexible. Their reading technique is varied to suit the occasion. They know that there are many kinds of reading, and they try to become skilled in all of them. Some materials demand a slow, analytical approach; insurance policies and contracts are good examples. Light fiction calls for a casual kind of reading at a fairly rapid rate. Another kind of material permits the reader to glance quickly down the column of print, snatching ideas on the run. This is called skimming.

Comprehension is another aspect of flexible reading. There are degrees or levels of comprehension that are appropriate for certain materials. For example, a very practical and thorough kind is needed to follow directions accurately. Obviously we don't need such thoroughness for reading the comics. Textbooks require the student to remember concepts and to understand relationships. The student, moreover, is expected to use comprehension as a tool for thinking. But simple articles of passing interest require only a temporary kind of comprehension.

We often run across articles, accounts, and stories that are of just casual or passing interest to us. These may be unrelated to school or the job; they may contain very little factual content; and they are very simply written. To read these materials analytically as we would read contracts, documents, and textbooks would be a waste of time. To use our study skills and techniques on them would be nonproductive and would be wasted effort. We need only to skim these materials to understand them.

1. Good readers _____ their reading technique to suit the occasion.

2. Light fiction calls for an informal kind of reading at a fairly _____ rate.

3. Textbooks should be read slowly because they require the student to remember _____ and understand relationships.

4. Simple articles of only passing interest need only to be _____ to be understood.

5. Because the passage from Malcolm X's autobiography is relatively easy to read, it does not have to be read quite as _____ as a textbook.

9 The Women of Brewster Place

Gloria Naylor

AUTHOR NOTES—
Gloria Naylor was born in New York City in 1950 and educated at Brooklyn College and Yale University. She began writing when she was still in college. Her first novel, *The Women of Brewster Place*, won the 1983 American Book Award for first fiction and was later made into a television movie by Oprah Winfrey. Since then she has published three other novels, *Linden Hills*, *Mama Day*, and *Bailey's Cafe*.

Naylor has lectured at various colleges and universities, including Brandeis, Cornell, and Princeton. In 1996 *Children of the Night*, a collection of stories by black writers that Naylor edited, was published. She is at work on *The Men of Brewster Place*, which will explore the male characters from her first novel.

VOCABULARY, PART ONE—
All of these terms are in the story you are about to read. Study each term and its meaning. Then answer the questions below.

As you read the story, notice how each term is used. You will have more questions about the terms later.

implications, suggestions; insinuations

assets, any possessions that are worth money

forfeit, to give up

bond, money paid to keep a person out of jail until he or she is brought to trial

savored, enjoyed the taste of

reveled, took great pleasure in

void, hollow space; emptiness

impregnable, unable to be broken through

repentant, sorry

disconcertedly, in an embarrassed way

1. Which term could describe a safe that crooks could not get into?

   _____

2. Which term might describe your feelings if you felt very bad about insulting your best friend? _____

3. Which term might a person use in talking about his house, his car, and his bank accounts? _____

4. Which term tells what your team might do if none of the members could be present for a game? _____

5. Which term could best describe the sensations you felt in your mouth while eating a delicious blueberry pie? _____

A READING PURPOSE—

In this selection a mother believes in her son and bails him out of jail. As you read, decide whether her support of him is justified.

■

1 The judge set bail the next day, and Basil was given an early trial date. Cecil Garvin tried to appeal the bail, but the court denied his plea.

2 "I'm sorry, Mrs. Michael, it's the best I could do. There's no need, really, to try and raise so much money. The case goes to trial in only two weeks, and it won't be a complicated proceeding. I've talked to the district attorney, and they won't push too heavily on the assault charge if we drop the <u>implications</u> of undue force in the arrest. So it's going to work out well for all the parties involved. And your son will be free in less than fifteen days."

3 "I still want to put up the bail," Mattie said.

4 Garvin looked worried. "It's a great deal of money, Mrs. Michael, and you don't have the ready <u>assets</u> for something like that."

5 "I've got my house; it's mine and paid for. Can't I put that up for bail?"

6 "Well, yes, but you do understand that bail is only posted to insure that the defendant appears for trial. If they don't appear, the court issues a bench warrant for the truant party and you <u>forfeit</u> your <u>bond</u>. You do understand that?"

7 "I understand."

8 The lawyer looked thoughtfully over at Basil. "It's only a matter of two weeks, Mrs. Michael. Some defendants spend months waiting for trial. Perhaps you should reconsider."

9 Mattie stared at him, and she thought about the blonde girl in the silver frame on his desk. "If it was your daughter locked up in a place like that," she said angrily, "could you stand there and say the same thing?"

10 His face reddened, and he stammered for a moment. "That's not what I mean, Mrs. Michael. It's just that with some people it's better to...well, it's up to you. It is your son, after all. Come along, and I'll give you the necessary papers to take to a bonding company."

11 The snow fell early that year. When Basil and Mattie left the precinct, the wide soft flakes were floating in gentle layers on the November air. Basil reached out and tried to grab one to give her, and he laughed as it melted in his hand.

12 "Remember how I used to cry when I tried to bring you a snowflake and it always disappeared?" He held his face up to the sky and let the snow fall on his closed lids. "Oh, God, Mama, isn't it beautiful?"

13 "Beautiful? You always hated the snow."

14 "Not now, it's wonderful. It's out here and free, like I am. I love it!" And he wrapped his arms around himself.

15 Mattie's insides expanded to take in his joy.

16 "And I love you, Mama." He put his arm around her shoulder and squeezed. "Thank you."

17 Mattie sucked her teeth and playfully shoved him away. "Thank me for what? Boy, go on and get the car before I catch my death of cold in all this beautiful snow of yours."

18 Mattie watched him as he moved through the parking lot almost singing, and she took in his happiness and made it her own just as she'd done with every emotion that had ever claimed him. She took in the sweetness of his freedom and let it roll around her tongue, while she <u>savored</u> its fragrant juices and allowed the syrupy fluid to coat her mouth and drip slowly down her throat.

19 She feasted on this sweetness during the next two weeks. Basil had been returned to her, and she <u>reveled</u> in his presence. He drove her to work in the mornings and would often be waiting when she got off. They cleaned the yard together and covered her shrubbery with burlap. They rearranged furniture and straightened the attic, and he even washed windows for her—a chore he had hated from childhood. There was no end to the things he did for her, and he stayed close to home. It was so good to have a nice home to come to, he told her. And she grew full from this nectar and allowed herself to dream again of the wife he would bring home and the grandchildren who would keep her spirit there.

20 The lawyer called at the end of the second week to remind them of the court appointment, and Basil grew irritable. He told her he hated the thought of that place. He had tried to pretend that it didn't exist, and he had been so happy. Now this. What if something went wrong and they kept him again? You couldn't trust those honky lawyers—what did they care about him? Those people in that bar weren't friends of his—what if they changed their stories? What if the girl hated him now and decided to lie? He remembered the way she had screamed over the dead man's body. Yes, she would lie to get back at him. He knew it.

21 "I'll blow my brains out before I spend my life in jail," he said to Mattie while driving her to work.

22 "Basil, stop talkin' stupidness!" Her voice was sharp. She had not been able to sleep well the last two nights, lying and listening to him pacing around in his room. "I've been hearing nothing but nonsense the last coupla days, and I'm sick of it."

23 "Nonsense!" He swung his head around.

24 "Yes, damned nonsense! You ain't going to jail 'cause you ain't done nothing to go to jail for. We go to court Tuesday; they'll give all the evidence, and you'll be clear. That's all there is to it. The lawyer said so, and he should know."

25 "Mama, he'll say anything to get your money. If someone offered him a nickel more than you paid, he'd throw me in jail personally and swallow the key. You don't know them like I do, and you don't know what it's like in those cells. And they'll send me to a worse place than some county jail." He looked at her sorrowfully. "I couldn't stand it, Mama. I just couldn't."

26 Mattie sighed, turned her head from him, and looked out the window. There was nothing to say. Whatever was lacking within him that made it impossible to confront the difficulties of life could not be supplied with words. She saw it now. There was a <u>void</u> in his being that had been padded and cushioned over the years, and now that covering had grown <u>impregnable</u>. She bit on her bottom lip and swallowed back a sob. God had given her what she prayed for—a little boy who would always need her.

27 She felt him looking at her turned head from time to time and knew he was puzzled by her silence. He was waiting to be coaxed and petted into a lighter mood, but she forced herself to keep staring out the window. When the car pulled up to her job, she mumbled a good-bye and reached for the latch. Basil grabbed her hand, leaned over, and kissed her cheek.

28 "Good-bye, Mama."

29 She was touched by the gentleness in his caress and immediately <u>repentant</u> of her attitude in the car. During the day she resolved to make amends to him. After all, he was under a great deal of pressure, and it wasn't fair that he bear it alone. Was it so wrong that he seemed to need her constant support? Had he not been trained to expect it? And he had been trying so hard those last two weeks; she couldn't let him down now. She would go home and make him a special dinner—creamed chicken with rice—he always loved that. Then they would sit and talk, and she would tell him, once again, or as many times as needed, that it was going to be all right.

30 Basil wasn't waiting for Mattie when she finished work, so she took the bus home and stopped by the store to pick up the things she needed for his dinner. She walked up the street and saw that his car wasn't parked out front and the house was dark. She stood for a moment by the front gate, first looking at the space where the car should be and then at the unlit windows. Normally she would have gone through the front door, taken off her coat, and hung it in the front hall closet. Tonight she entered the house through the back door that led straight into the kitchen. She took off her coat and

laid it on one of the kitchen chairs. There was an extra jacket of his in the front hall closet that would not be there.

> Basil was Mattie's well-loved son. Could she sacrifice everything—even her house—for him?

31 She washed her hands at the sink and immediately started to cut up the chicken and peel and slice vegetables. Her feet were beginning to ache, but her house slippers were in the living room, under a table where his portable radio would not be, so she limped around her kitchen while finishing his dinner. She let the water run in the sink longer than necessary and dropped her knife and set the pots on the stove with a fraction of extra force. She made as much noise as she could to ward off the stillness of the upstairs bedroom that kept trying to creep into her kitchen, carrying empty drawers and closets, a vacant space where a suitcase had lain, missing toothpaste. She banged pot lids and beat sauces in aluminum bowls until her arms were tired. She watched and fussed over his dinner, opening and closing the oven door a dozen times—anything to keep back the stillness until he would drive up in his car, say he had come to his senses, sit down and eat her creamed chicken, save a lifetime of work lying in the bricks of her home.

32 The vegetables were done, the chicken almost burnt, and the biscuits had to come out of the oven. She turned off the gas jets, opened the oven door, and banged the pan of biscuits onto the counter top. She looked frantically at the creeping shadows over her kitchen door and rushed to the cabinet and took out plates and silverware. She slammed the cabinet shut and slowly and noisily set the table for two. She looked pleadingly around the kitchen, but there was nothing left to be done. So she pulled out the kitchen chair, letting the metal legs drag across the tiles. Trembling, she sat down, put her head in her hands, and waited for the patient and crouching stillness just beyond the kitchen door.

33 A hand touched her shoulder, and Mattie gave a small cry.

34 "Didn't mean to startle you, mam, but it's snowing pretty bad, and we gotta move this stuff upstairs. Would you please go up and unlock the door?"

35 At first Mattie looked vacantly into the face of the man and then her mind snapped into place from its long stretch over time. The cab had just backed out of Brewster Place, and she watched it turn down the avenue and drive away. Her eyes trailed slowly along the cracked stoops and snowfilled gutters until they come to her building. She glanced at the walls and, with an inner sigh, remembered her plants again.

36 The mover who had addressed her was staring at her uncomfortably.

37 "Oh, yes, I'm sorry," she said disconcertedly. "I have the keys right here, don't I?" And she opened her pocketbook and started searching for them.

38 The two men looked at each other, and one shrugged his shoulders and pointed his finger toward his head.

39 Mattie grasped the cold metal key in one hand and put the other on the iron railing and climbed the stoop to the front entrance. As she opened the door and entered the dingy hallway, a snowflake caught in her collar, melted, and rolled down her back like a frozen tear.

Starting Time	
Reading Time	
Finishing Time	
■ Reading Rate	

COMPREHENSION —

Read the following questions and statements. For each one, put an X in the box before the option that contains the most complete or accurate answer.

1. This story takes place in
   - ☐ a. November.
   - ☐ b. December.
   - ☐ c. January.
   - ☐ d. February.

2. The lawyer expects that Basil will
   - ☐ a. stay with Mattie.
   - ☐ b. commit another crime.
   - ☐ c. leave town.
   - ☐ d. pay the bond money back to Mattie.

3. The last seven paragraphs are set off from the rest of the story to show that
   - [ ] a. the time is coming for Basil to return.
   - [ ] b. Mattie is remembering the past.
   - [ ] c. a day or two has gone by.
   - [ ] d. a month or two has gone by.

4. The main point that the events in this story lead to is that
   - [ ] a. parents can never do enough for their children.
   - [ ] b. sometimes parents do too much for their children.
   - [ ] c. it's hard for a mother to raise a child alone.
   - [ ] d. women tend to be more self-sacrificing than men.

5. When Basil is released from jail, he hugs himself, then hugs his mother. From this you can conclude that he is
   - [ ] a. grateful.
   - [ ] b. forgetful.
   - [ ] c. self-centered.
   - [ ] d. sorry.

6. When Mattie goes home and begins cooking the dinner, she knows Basil is gone because
   - [ ] a. he was still angry about their argument.
   - [ ] b. he was guilty of the crime he was charged with.
   - [ ] c. it fits with what she has figured out about his character.
   - [ ] d. he has other friends he can stay with.

7. At the end of the story, Mattie is crying because
   - [ ] a. she is alone in the cold.
   - [ ] b. Basil has still not contacted her.
   - [ ] c. she feels like a fool.
   - [ ] d. she has lost her house.

8. The tone the author uses in presenting Mattie is one of
   - [ ] a. mockery.
   - [ ] b. sympathy.
   - [ ] c. anger.
   - [ ] d. unconcern.

9. Basil is a person who
   - [ ] a. would take things more seriously if he had more money.
   - [ ] b. needs constant attention.
   - [ ] c. never takes responsibility for his actions.
   - [ ] d. needs someone to provide structure in his life.

10. When the author says of Mattie, "She took in the sweetness of his freedom and let it roll around her tongue, while she savored its fragrant juices," she is using
    - [ ] a. a symbol.
    - [ ] b. an exaggeration.
    - [ ] c. a simile.
    - [ ] d. a metaphor.

Comprehension Skills
1. recalling specific facts
2. retaining concepts
3. organizing facts
4. understanding the main idea
5. drawing a conclusion
6. making a judgment
7. making an inference
8. recognizing tone
9. understanding characters
10. appreciating literary forms

VOCABULARY, PART TWO—
Write the term that makes the most sense in each sentence.

repentant   implications
bond   assets
reveled

1. Mattie was willing to sacrifice all her
   _____ to pay Basil's way out of jail.

2. Basil had made _____ that there was undue force used in his arrest, but the lawyer questioned whether these were true.

3. By paying his _____, Mattie showed she believed Basil would stay around for his trial.

4. Mattie was delighted to have Basil at home and _____ in his company.

5. She wanted to believe he was _____ about the problems he had caused her.

disconcertedly   void

forfeit   impregnable

savored

6. Mattie had tried to shower Basil with good influences, but she could see he had a

_____ within him that could never be filled.

7. She tried to reason with him but felt that he put up a wall between them that was

_____.

8. Mattie was embarrassed after their argument and tried _____ to make things up to him.

9. She cooked him a special meal with foods he had always _____ .

10. In the end, she had to _____ her house because he ran out on the bond money.

Comprehension Score   ☐

Vocabulary Score   ☐

WRITING —
At what point did you know what Basil was going to do? What clues in the story led you to your conclusion? Write a few paragraphs explaining how you figured things out. Use examples from the text to support your ideas.

STUDY SKILLS —
Read the following passage and answer the questions that follow it.

Skimming for Facts
Skimming is an art and a skill—it is not careless reading.

STUDY-TYPE MATERIAL
One kind of material that the reader can skim effectively is study-type material in order to locate certain facts or

to extract specific data. Actually this type of reading is a reference skill—skimming through a chapter or lesson to see if a particular topic is discussed. When the student finds what he or she is looking for, other reading and study techniques can then be used. Consider this type of skimming a more thorough kind of previewing.

When skimming for facts, here is how to proceed.

1. Read the Title. This may tell you if the author's subject is one that might include the information you need.

2. Read the Subhead. Be alert for a word pertaining to your topic. See if the author announces a category or classification that might include it.

3. Read the Illustration. Look for graphic information relating to what you are seeking.

4. Read First Sentences. Look for paragraphs that contain information and definitions. These are the ones most likely to contain factual data. Skim through these, looking for your topic. Paragraphs of introduction may tell you that what you are seeking is coming next. Paragraphs of illustration will probably not contain factual data—these may be glossed over or skipped entirely. The closing paragraph is not likely to help, either.

Skimming for facts is a valuable reference skill and one more tool for the flexible reader.

1. Skimming is an art and a skill—it is not

_____ reading.

2. One kind of material that permits the reader to skim is _____ matter in which the student locates certain facts.

3. Reading the _____ may tell you if the author's subject contains information that you need.

4. Look for paragraphs that contain information and

_____.

5. If you had a feeling that Basil might not be around at the end of the selection you just read, you might quickly _____ the last few paragraphs to see if your suspicions were true.

10 | My American Journey

Colin Powell

AUTHOR NOTES—
Colin Powell was born in New York City of Jamaican parents. After graduating from college in 1958, he joined the army, rising through the ranks to become a four-star general. He has served in various posts in the government, including assistant to President George Bush for national security affairs. In 1989 he became chairman of the military Joint Chiefs of Staff, holding that post until 1993. In 1994 he retired from the military.

In the 1996 presidential election Powell was widely sought as a candidate; however, he declined to run. In 1997 he became an organizer of a nationwide movement promoting individual and corporate volunteer efforts to help poor children.

My American Journey, Powell's autobiography, was published in 1995.

VOCABULARY, PART ONE—
All of these terms are in the story you are about to read. Study each term and its meaning. Then answer the questions below.

As you read the story, notice how each term is used. You will have more questions about the terms later.

marathon, very lengthy

patronized, been a customer of; used

reviled, called bad names

hounded, chased away

obsessed, made anxious; haunted

fruitlessly, unsuccessfully

resounding, impressive; enthusiastically spoken

equestrian, on horseback

immortalize, to make live forever

archives, a place where public documents and records are kept

1. Which term could describe a statue of General Grant riding a horse?

   _____

2. Which term names a place where you might be able to find a copy of your birth certificate? _____

3. Which term could describe a meeting that goes on for six hours?

   _____

4. Which term could describe your dealings with a problem that you think about almost every minute of the day? _____

5. What might you be trying to do for your mother if you wrote a book about her so no one would forget her? _____

A R E A D I N G P U R P O S E —

In this selection Powell describes his efforts to honor black military heroes who came before him. Read to see how he originally got interested in this project.

_____

■

1 One afternoon in September, I slipped out of a marathon briefing on Army communications and came home early. "Colin," Alma said, "you need a haircut." I had not done that well at the post barbershop and managed to dredge up from my memory a shop in the black section of Leavenworth that I had patronized fourteen years before. I drove downtown, and there was the shop, just as I remembered it, down to the striped barber pole in front. Inside, faded pinups advertising ancient hair tonics covered the wall. Dog-eared magazines littered a rack, and the place had that unique barbershop fragrance. The shop was empty except for a barber older than his posters.

2 He put down his newspaper and waved me to a chair. "Welcome, General," he said, introducing himself as "Old Sarge" and draping a striped sheet over me. As he snipped away, I studied the photographs over the mirror, black generals, including Rock Cartwright, Julius Becton, Roscoe Robinson, Emmet Paige, and Harry Brooks, all from the generation just ahead of me. The barber handed me a small red-covered diary. "I'm going to ask you to sign my book when we're done," he said. The cover was stamped "1959." I started thumbing through it, studying the signatures, caught up in the parade of familiar names. His little red book read like black military history. Early signatures were mostly of majors, then a few lieutenant colonels, and in more recent years, a comforting number of more senior officers. And then I stopped short. There, in 1968, I found "Colin Powell, Major, USA." I had no recollection of signing the book.

3 "You don't remember me," Old Sarge said, "but I remember you."

4 He held up a hand mirror so I could see the back of my head. I nodded my approval. He removed the sheet and shook it out. I fished out a pen and signed the book, this time as "Brigadier General Powell." "What's your name again?" I asked.

5 "Jalester Linton," he said, "10th Cavalry, Buffalo Soldiers."

6 I was not only reading black military history, I was shaking its hand. We got to talking about all the sites on the post named for fabled soldiers of the past, like Grant Avenue and Eisenhower Hall. I asked Old Sarge if anything at Leavenworth commemorated the Buffalo Soldiers. "Well," Linton said, "there's 9th and 10th Cavalry avenues." I had never heard of them.

7 I became curious about the history of the Buffalo Soldiers. I started reading everything I could lay my hands on. What I learned filled me with pride at the feats these black men had achieved and with sadness at the injustices and neglect they had suffered. Blacks had fought in just about all of America's

wars. They served to prove themselves the equal of white soldiers, which was precisely why some whites did not want blacks in uniform. My reading led me to the words of Howell Cobb, a Confederate general, who advised Jefferson Davis against arming blacks. "Use all negroes you can get for...cooking, digging, chopping and such," Cobb said, "But don't arm them. If slaves will make good soldiers," he warned, "our whole theory of slavery is wrong." Frederick Douglass put it another way: "Once you let the black man get upon his person the brass letters 'U.S.,' let him get an eagle on his button and bullets in his pocket, and there is no power on earth which can deny he has earned the right to citizenship in the United States."

> The Buffalo Soldiers had fought bravely and honorably. They deserved a fitting monument, and Colin Powell was going to help them get it.

8   In 1867, Congress officially put that eagle on the buttons and put bullets in the pockets when it created four black regiments. For twenty-two years, a white officer, Colonel Benjamin H. Grierson, commanded one of them, the 10th Cavalry. When Grierson finally bid goodbye to his troops, he said, "The valuable service to their country cannot fail, sooner or later, to meet with due recognition and reward." Ninety-five years later, it was too late for reward, and I did not see much recognition of the Buffalo Soldiers either.

9   I read about the fate of Lieutenant Henry O. Flipper. Imagine a child born into slavery, yet possessing the grit to get himself admitted to the U.S. Military Academy in 1873, just ten years after Emancipation. Every black cadet before Flipper had been shunned, reviled, and ultimately hounded from West Point. Flipper took it all for four years without breaking and graduated in 1877. He was sent out West in 1878 to join Troop A, 10th Cavalry, the first black officer ever assigned to the Buffalo Soldiers. Three years later, bigots in uniform framed him on a charge of embezzling from commissary funds. A court-martial found Flipper innocent of that charge, but guilty of "conduct unbecoming an officer and a gentleman." He was given a dishonorable discharge, his military career in ruins by age twenty-five. The resilient Flipper nevertheless managed to carve out successful careers as a mining engineer, author, and newspaper editor. But the stain on his honor obsessed him, and he spent the final years of his life fruitlessly trying to clear his name. The finding of the court-martial was finally reversed in 1976 through the determined efforts of a white schoolteacher from Georgia named Ray MacColl.

10   During the court-martial, Flipper's attorney had put the question squarely: "Whether it is possible for a colored man to secure and hold a position as an officer of the Army?" My own career and that of thousands of other black officers answered with a resounding yes. But we knew that the path through the underbrush of prejudice and discrimination had been cleared by the sacrifices of nameless blacks who had gone before us, the Old Sarges and Henry Flippers. To them we owed everything.

11   Not long after my visit to the barbershop, I was jogging past the post cemetery and came upon an abandoned trailer park. Nothing was left but crumbling concrete platforms and an intersection of gravel roads. There I saw a leaning, weather-beaten street sign marking 9th Cavalry Avenue and another marking 10th Cavalry Avenue. I was still upset when I got back to my quarters. I took a shower, went to my office, and called in the post historian, retired Colonel Robert von Schlemmer. "Is that the best we can do?" I said. "Two dirt roads in an abandoned trailer park?"

12   "Sir, you're right," von Schlemmer said patiently. "But before you blow a gasket, you should know what I went through just to get the Buffalo Soldiers even that recognition."

13   "Fine," I said, "but where do we go from here? I want something more appropriate honoring the memory of those men."

14   "I'll tell you what," he said. "If you'll take the lead, I'll get the Leavenworth Historical Society behind you, and we'll throw in some seed money, maybe five thousand dollars. But you've got to figure out what you want to do."

15   I had been thinking about it all morning. "Leavenworth is full of equestrian statues," I pointed out. "I'd like to see a statue here honoring the Buffalo Soldiers. It ought to stand on the bluff overlooking the Missouri, with the cavalryman facing west, headed for the future."

16   Five thousand dollars was not going to produce much of a statue, von Schlemmer warned. The first thing I was going to have to learn was how to raise money.

17   I believed I had a duty to those black troops who had eased my way. Building a memorial to the Buffalo Soldiers became my personal crusade. I called in Captain Phil Coker, Hudachek's former aide, whom I

had brought from Fort Carson. "You're 10th Cavalry, aren't you?" I asked Phil. Yes, Coker said, he had been part of the squadron at Fort Carson, obviously long after the 10th had been integrated, which occurred during the Korean War. "You're going to im-mortalize your old outfit," I told him. "You're going to dig up the history of the Buffalo Soldiers." Coker went at it as if we were talking about *his* ancestors. He scoured the archives while I started looking for money. Those troops had suffered second-class treatment after serving as first-class fighting men.

I was determined that the Buffalo Soldiers were finally going to go first-class.

Starting Time ☐

Reading Time ☐

Finishing Time ☐

■ Reading Rate ☐

COMPREHENSION —

Read the following questions and statements. For each one, put an X in the box before the option that contains the most complete or accurate answer.

1. Powell got his inspiration for the Buffalo Soldiers' statue from his
   ☐ a. barber.
   ☐ b. wife.
   ☐ c. office assistant.
   ☐ d. superior officer.

2. Ninth and 10th Cavalry Avenues were, according to Powell,
   ☐ a. formerly paved but are now dirt roads.
   ☐ b. not much of a memorial.
   ☐ c. all you could expect of a white-dominated army.
   ☐ d. roads that should be expanded and be given elaborate street signs.

3. The events described in this story move
   ☐ a. in strict chronological order.
   ☐ b. in strict spatial order.
   ☐ c. between the present and the future.
   ☐ d. between the present and the past.

4. A good title for this selection would be
   ☐ a. The Anger of a Righteous Man.
   ☐ b. The Beginning of a Crusade.
   ☐ c. A History of the Buffalo Soldiers.
   ☐ d. The Sad Results of Bigotry.

5. Powell found more high-ranking officers in the later pages of the diary because
   ☐ a. more blacks were being promoted to higher jobs.
   ☐ b. Old Sarge's business was getting better.
   ☐ c. the pages were organized consecutively according to the signers' ranks.
   ☐ d. blacks were becoming prouder of their role in the military.

6. Colonel von Schlemmer had become involved with the Buffalo Soldiers
   ☐ a. only when Powell demanded it.
   ☐ b. at the insistence of other black officers in the camp.
   ☐ c. in his role as camp historian.
   ☐ d. as a member of the Leavenworth Historical Society.

7. Powell wanted to honor the Buffalo Soldiers
   ☐ a. so that whites would learn about them.
   ☐ b. for the sake of Lieutenant Henry O. Flipper.
   ☐ c. for the sake of all blacks in the military.
   ☐ d. because Old Sarge had shamed him into it.

8. In describing the fate of Lieutenant Flipper, Powell's tone is
   ☐ a. very angry.
   ☐ b. calmly accepting.
   ☐ c. righteously upset.
   ☐ d. extremely matter-of-fact.

9. In this selection Powell shows himself as
   ☐ a. short-tempered.
   ☐ b. determined.
   ☐ c. bossy.
   ☐ d. talkative.

10. This selection is
    ☐ a. a folk tale.
    ☐ b. a fictional story.
    ☐ c. a biography.
    ☐ d. an autobiography.

Comprehension Skills
1. recalling specific facts
2. retaining concepts

58

3. organizing facts
4. understanding the main idea
5. drawing a conclusion
6. making a judgment
7. making an inference
8. recognizing tone
9. understanding characters
10. appreciating literary forms

VOCABULARY, PART TWO —

Write the term that makes the most sense in each sentence.

patronized   **hounded**
fruitlessly   **resounding**
immortalize

1. Rather than let the Buffalo Soldiers be forgotten, Powell would _____ them with a statue in their honor.

2. Powell had been in Old Sarge's barbershop many years earlier, but he hadn't _____ the place for quite a long time.

3. Powell _____ tried to remember signing Old Sarge's book, but he just could not recall doing it.

4. Many of the Buffalo Soldiers had been _____ and otherwise insulted by white soldiers.

5. Powell made a _____ promise that he would find a way to honor these soldiers.

marathon   **reviled**
obsessed   **equestrian**
archives

6. Once Powell decided to erect the statue, he couldn't stop thinking about it; he was _____ with the idea.

7. He considered calling a(n) _____ meeting of his staff, where they could discuss his plan for hours.

8. A(n) _____ statue was appropriate because as cavalry, the early Buffalo Soldiers typically were on horseback.

9. The statue would in some way pay back the soldiers who had been _____ by their white associates.

10. Looking in the _____ was a good way to find details of the Buffalo Soldiers' history.

Comprehension Score   [   ]

Vocabulary Score   [   ]

WRITING —

Take on the role of Colin Powell and write a brief letter to your congressional representative requesting support for a statue honoring the Buffalo Soldiers. Include details from this story to show why the statue is needed.

STUDY SKILLS —

Read the following passage and answer the questions that follow it.

Dynamic Skimming

One type of high-speed skimming can be labeled dynamic skimming. The label *dynamic* is appropriate because of the impressive results this kind of skimming yields at such high speeds. The steps to dynamic skimming are these.

1. Preview. As you no doubt have begun to realize, previewing is necessary in any kind of reading. In dynamic skimming, previewing is more essential than ever. Before skimming, the reader must perform a thorough and comprehensive preview of the entire article. The steps to previewing do not change. It's just that more time is spent on previewing to form a clear mental outline of the article for skimming.

2. Skim. This time let your eyes flow down the column of print, snatching ideas on the run. Do not stop to read—do not pause to reflect. Strive to let the words trigger your thinking as you skim by.

This kind of skimming is difficult at first because most readers have been in the habit of reading line by line. To overcome this natural tendency, use your finger as a pacer to force your eyes down the page. You may wish to move your finger in a zigzag fashion, letting the eyes fixate (stop and read) twice on each line. Gradually speed up until you are able to cover the page in 10 or 12 seconds.

3. Reread. This is the third step to dynamic skimming. Rereading is done like previewing, as you attempt to fill gaps in your understanding of the article.

To be successful, you must have easy material and perform each of the three steps: preview, skim, and reread.

1. High-speed skimming is called _____ skimming.

2. _____, the first step, is necessary for reading of any kind.

3. While skimming, the second step, your eyes flow down the column of print, snatching _____ on the run.

4. Following these steps with Powell's selection would have revealed that Powell included several paragraphs on the _____ of the Buffalo Soldiers.

5. Through _____, the third step, you would have learned something of Powell's plans to have a statue erected.

11 The Autobiography of My Mother

Jamaica Kincaid

AUTHOR NOTES—
Jamaica Kincaid was born in St. John's in Antigua, an island in the Caribbean. She came to the United States when she was 18 and presently lives with her family in Vermont.

Kincaid's first book, the short story collection *At the Bottom of the River*, was published in 1983 and nominated for the PEN/Faulkner Award. Other fictional works, which all show the influence of her life in the West Indies, include *Annie John* (1985), *Lucy* (1991), and *The Autobiography of My Mother* (1996). Kincaid has been employed as a staff writer at *The New Yorker* magazine for many years.

VOCABULARY, PART ONE—

All of these terms are in the story you are about to read. Study each term and its meaning. Then answer the questions below.

As you read the story, notice how each term is used. You will have more questions about the terms later.

flamboyant, flashy; showy

clarity, clearness

antecedents, events or occurrences that came earlier

self-loathing, self-hatred

birthright, privileges that a person receives through birth

patois, a regional form of a language, different from the standard form

retrieve, to recover or bring back

diurnal, happening every day; daily

porous, able to be saturated by water

lagoon, a small lake attached to another body of water

1. Which term names a place where you might sail a boat?

    _____

2. Which term could describe an outfit consisting of a bright orange T-shirt and lime-colored slacks? _____

3. Which term describes the condition of sand on a beach?

    _____

4. What condition might a person be suffering from if he only says terrible things about himself? _____

5. Which term describes what you do when you throw something into the garbage and then go and take it back out? _____

A READING PURPOSE—

This selection describes a period in the life of a young girl. As you read, try to form an impression of what the girl is like.

■

1   It was my father's wish that I be sent to school. It was an unusual request; girls did not attend school, none of Ma Eunice's girl children attended school. I shall never know what made him do such a thing. I can only imagine that he desired such a thing for me without giving it too much thought, because in the end what could an education do for someone like me? I can only say what I did not have; I can only measure it against what I did have and find misery in the difference. And yet, and yet...it was for this reason that I came to see for the first time what lay beyond the path that led away from my house. And I can so well remember the feel of the cloth of my skirt and blouse—coarse because it was new—a green skirt and beige blouse, a uniform, its colors and style mimicking the colors and style of a school somewhere else, somewhere far away; and I had on a pair of brown thick cloth shoes and brown cotton socks which my father had gotten for me, I did not know where. And to mention that I did not know where these things came from, to say that I wondered about them, is really to say that this was the first time I had worn such things as shoes and socks, and they caused my feet to ache and swell and the skin to blister and break, but I was made to wear them until my feet got used to them, and my feet—all of me—did. That morning was a morning like any other, so ordinary it was profound: it was

sunny in some places and not in others, and the two (sunny, cloudy) occupied different parts of the sky quite comfortably; there was the green of the leaves, the red burst of the flowers from the <u>flamboyant</u> trees, the sickly yellow fruit of the cashew, the smell of lime, the smell of almonds, the coffee on my breath, Eunice's skirt blowing in my face, and the stirring up of the smells that came from between her legs, which I shall never forget, and whenever I smell myself I am reminded of her. The river was low, so I did not hear the sound of the water rushing over stones; the breeze was soft, so the leaves did not rustle in the trees.

2   I had these sensations of seeing, smelling, and hearing on my journey down the path on the way to my school. When I reached the road and placed my newly shod feet on it, this was the first time I had done so. I was aware of this. It was a road of small stones and tightly packed dirt, and each step I took was awkward; the ground shifted, my feet slipped backward. The road stretched out ahead of me and vanished around a bend; we kept walking toward this bend and then we came to the bend and the bend gave way to more of the same road and then another bend. We came to my school before the end of the last bend. It was a small building with one door and four windows; it had a wooden floor; there was a small reptile crawling along a beam in the

roof; there were three long desks lined up one behind the other; there was a large wooden table and a chair facing the three long desks; on the wall

> When the narrator goes to school for the first time, many of the ways in which she sees the world change.

behind the wooden table and chair was a map; at the top of the map were the words "THE BRITISH EMPIRE." These were the first words I learned to read.

3 In that room always there were only boys; I did not sit in a schoolroom with other girls until I was older. I was not afraid in that new situation: I did not know how to be that then and do not know how to be that now. I was not afraid, because my mother had already died and that is the only thing a child is really afraid of; when I was born, my mother was dead, and I had already lived all those years with Eunice, a woman who was not my mother and who could not love me, and without my father, never knowing when I would see him again, so I was not afraid for myself in this situation. (And if it is not really true that I was not afraid then, it was not the only time that I did not admit to myself my own vulnerability.)

4 If I speak now of those first days with clarity and insight, it is not an invention, it should not surprise; at the time, each thing as it took place stood out in my mind with a sharpness that I now take for granted; it did not then have a meaning, it did not have a context, I did not yet know the history of events, I did not know their antecedents. My teacher was a woman who had been trained by Methodist missionaries; she was of the African people, that I could see, and she found in this a source of humiliation and self-loathing, and she wore despair like an article of clothing, like a mantle, or a staff on which she leaned constantly, a birthright which she would pass on to us. She did not love us; we did not love her; we did not love one another, not then, not ever. There were seven boys and myself. The boys, too, were all African people. My teacher and these boys looked at me and looked at me: I had thick eyebrows; my hair was coarse, thick, and wavy; my eyes were set far apart from each other and they had the shape of almonds; my lips were wide and narrow in an unexpected way. I was of the African people, but not exclusively. My mother was a Carib woman, and when they looked at me this is what

they saw: The Carib people had been defeated and then exterminated, thrown away like the weeds in a garden; the African people had been defeated but had survived. When they looked at me, they saw only the Carib people. They were wrong but I did not tell them so.

5 I started to speak quite openly then—to myself frequently, to others only when it was absolutely necessary. We spoke English in school—proper English, not patois—and among ourselves we spoke French patois, a language that was not considered proper at all, a language that a person from France could not speak and could only with difficulty understand. I spoke to myself because I grew to like the sound of my own voice. It had a sweetness to me, it made my loneliness less, for I was lonely and wished to see people in whose faces I could recognize something of myself. Because who was I? My mother was dead; I had not seen my father for a long time.

6 I learned to read and write very quickly. My memory, my ability to retain information, to retrieve the tiniest detail, to recall who said what and when, was regarded as unusual, so unusual that my teacher, who was trained to think only of good and evil and whose judgment of such things was always mistaken, said I was evil, I was possessed— and to establish that there could be no doubt of this, she pointed again to the fact that my mother was of the Carib people.

7 My world then—silent, soft, and vegetable-like in its vulnerability, subject to the powerful whims of others, diurnal, beginning with the pale opening of light on the horizon each morning and ending with the sudden onset of dark at the beginning of each night—was both a mystery to me and the source of much pleasure: I loved the face of a gray sky, porous, grainy, wet, following me to school for mornings on end, sending down on me soft arrows of water; the face of that same sky when it was a hard, unsheltering blue, a backdrop for a cruel sun; the harsh heat that eventually became a part of me, like my blood; the overbearing trees (the stems of some of them the size of small trunks) that grew without restraint, as if beauty were only size, and I could tell them all apart by closing my eyes and listening to the sound the leaves made when they rubbed together; and I loved that moment when the white flowers from the cedar tree started to fall to the ground with a silence that I could hear, their petals at first still fresh, a soft kiss of pink and white, then a day later, crushed, wilted, and brown, a nuisance to the eye; and the river that had

become a small <u>lagoon</u> when one day on its own it changed course, on whose bank I would sit and watch families of birds, and frogs laying their eggs, and the sky turning from black to blue and blue to black, and rain falling on the sea beyond the lagoon but not on the mountain that was beyond the sea. It was while sitting in this place that I first began to dream about my mother; I had fallen asleep on the stones that covered the ground around me, my small body sinking into this surface as if it were feathers. I saw my mother come down a ladder. She wore a long white gown, the hem of it falling just above her heels, and that was all of her that was exposed, just her heels; she came down and down, but no more of her was ever revealed. Only her heels,

and the hem of her gown. At first I longed to see more, and then I became satisfied just to see her heels coming down toward me. When I awoke, I was not the same child I had been before I fell asleep. I longed to see my father and to be in his presence constantly.

Starting Time	
Reading Time	
Finishing Time	
■ Reading Rate	

COMPREHENSION —

Read the following questions and statements. For each one, put an X in the box before the option that contains the most complete or accurate answer.

1. This story takes place
   - ☐ a. just outside a medium-sized city.
   - ☒ b. entirely within a small town.
   - ☐ c. in the tropics.
   - ☐ d. along the slopes of a mountain.

2. The setting of the story is important because it
   - ☐ a. is something the narrator has to struggle against.
   - ☐ b. makes a vivid impression on the narrator.
   - ☐ c. shows how the British oppressed the native people.
   - ☒ d. shows the difference between Africans and Caribs.

3. The content of the story is mostly made up of
   - ☒ a. thoughts and impressions.
   - ☐ b. events.
   - ☐ c. disagreements and conflicts.
   - ☐ d. conversations and other dialogue.

4. A good summary of what this story is about is
   - ☐ a. how beautiful the natural world is.
   - ☒ b. how discrimination can weaken a person's resolve.
   - ☐ c. how a lonely child adjusts to going to school.
   - ☐ d. how fathers should not abandon their children.

5. Words that would best describe the narrator are
   - ☐ a. lonely and unpleasant.
   - ☐ b. intelligent and observant.
   - ☒ c. bitter and set in her ways.
   - ☐ d. inexperienced and sad.

6. The narrator probably only sees her mother's feet in the dream because
   - ☒ a. her mother seems to be floating in a cloud.
   - ☐ b. her mother wants the narrator to become closer to her father.
   - ☒ c. she had no clear image of what her mother actually looked like.
   - ☐ d. dreams are often quite different from reality.

7. The narrator mentions that "The British Empire" is the first thing she learns to read in order to show
   - ☐ a. how quickly she could learn difficult words.
   - ☒ b. that the empire was supposed to be an important part of people's lives.
   - ☐ c. where the African instructor had learned to read.
   - ☐ d. that her homeland was so intolerable to her that she wanted to escape to Britain.

8. The overall tone of this story is one of
   - ☐ a. love.
   - ☐ b. anger.
   - ☐ c. sadness.
   - ☒ d. loneliness.

9. The African instructor can best be described as
   - ☑ a. kindly and helpful.
   - ☐ b. sad and depressed.
   - ☐ c. narrow and bigoted.
   - ☐ d. intelligent but selfish.

10. The kind of narrator used in this story is
    - ☐ a. third person limited.
    - ☐ b. third person omniscient.
    - ☑ c. first person.
    - ☐ d. second person.

Comprehension Skills

1. recalling specific facts
2. retaining concepts
3. organizing facts
4. understanding the main idea
5. drawing a conclusion
6. making a judgment
7. making an inference
8. recognizing tone
9. understanding characters
10. appreciating literary forms

VOCABULARY, PART TWO—

Write the term that makes the most sense in each sentence.

antecedents   self-loathing
birthright   flamboyant
diurnal

1. The young girl liked the _____ things in nature, such as trees with bright red flowers.

2. She did not believe it was her _____ to get an education; rather, it was an advantage that her father wanted to give to her.

3. Perhaps because the teacher was filled with _____, she seemed to hate many of the students too.

4. The young girl was concerned mostly with the present and the _____ happenings that made up her life.

5. She did not worry about the history of events or what their _____ were.

clarity   retrieve
patois   porous
lagoon

6. Outside of school the children would speak a French _____ rather than the standard form of the language.

7. Sometimes they would go to the nearby _____ and sail paper boats in its clear waters.

8. If a boat sailed too far out, someone would swim out to _____ it.

9. At times the sky looked very _____, as if water were about to saturate it.

10. These events seemed printed on the narrator's brain and later she could remember them with great _____.

Comprehension Score [   ]

Vocabulary Score [   ]

WRITING—

How do you think the narrator gets along with the other students in her class? Write a few paragraphs that explain what you think. Use information from the story to support what you say.

STUDY SKILLS—

Read the following passage and answer the questions that follow it.

Building Vocabulary

There is a vital connection between language and learning ability and between good grades and the ability to communicate your thoughts clearly and accurately.

An academic curriculum incorporates many subjects, each of which is characterized by its own vocabulary of specialized terms. These terms must be understood if the subject is to be mastered.

All teachers, when evaluating and grading students, reward those who can express their understanding of key concepts and fundamental facts clearly and concisely. Students display this kind of understanding through their use of appropriate terminology. Thus, familiarity with the vocabulary of a subject opens the avenues of communication between student and instructor.

This is not to say that random flaunting of specialized terms will deceive instructors, but it stands to reason that as you acquire the vocabulary of a subject, you will also be accumulating fundamental knowledge in that field. This growth of vocabulary becomes the base on which new knowledge is acquired and assimilated during your regular study.

Familiar material is more easily read and understood than new material. This fact explains why we all tend to read articles in our field of interest with ease; we already have the necessary background of information. It also explains why we sometimes find new subjects dull and uninteresting. Learning the basic vocabulary of a subject gives us a foundation to build on and assures that our study of that field will be profitable.

1. The specialized vocabulary of a subject must be understood if the subject is to be _____.

2. Knowledge of vocabulary enables a student to express his or her _____ of the key concepts of a subject.

3. Acquiring a specific vocabulary also adds to fundamental _____ in a particular field.

4. Sometimes new subjects seem dull and uninteresting because we do not have the necessary _____ of information.

5. For example, if you did not know what Kincaid meant when she said she found it easy to *retrieve* facts, you would not understand that she had a good _____ for what she had learned.

12

The Heart of a Woman

Maya Angelou

AUTHOR NOTES—
Maya Angelou is best known for her series of autobiographies, which began in 1970 with *I Know Why the Caged Bird Sings. Heart of a Woman* (1981) is the fourth volume in the series. She has published children's books and numerous volumes of poetry, as well as a book of meditations, *Wouldn't Take Nothing for My Shoes*, (1993).

Angelou has also worked as an actress, dancer, scriptwriter, lecturer, and musician. She wrote the screenplay and musical score for the film *Georgia, Georgia* in 1972 and received an Emmy nomination for best supporting actress for her performance in the 1977 television series *Roots*.

She has been awarded more than a dozen honorary degrees and a place in the Black Filmmakers Hall of Fame. On January 20, 1993, Angelou read her poem, "On the Pulse of Morning," at the U.S. presidential inauguration ceremonies, becoming the first African American to be honored with that distinction.

VOCABULARY, PART ONE—
All of these terms are in the story you are about to read. Study each term and its meaning. Then answer the questions below.

As you read the story, notice how each term is used. You will have more questions about the terms later.

reverberated, echoed

perversity, abnormality

studiously, thoughtfully

taut, tightly drawn; tense; nervous

keen, sharp; piercing

rasp, harsh, grating sound

deprecating, disapproving

facetious, humorous; amusing

relish, enthusiasm

milling, moving around in confusion

1. Which term could be used to name the noise of a piece of chalk scratching on a blackboard? _____

2. Which term could describe a statement that everyone laughed at?

   _____

3. How might you be acting if you carefully considered all the possibilities in a situation? _____

4. How would you describe the comments of someone who always seemed to cut to the heart of a situation? _____

5. Which term might describe a rope that had no slack in it?

   _____

A READING PURPOSE —

In this selection Angelou describes an unnerving event from her early days as a writer. As you read, try to put yourself in her position and experience the emotions she feels.

■

1 The Harlem Writers Guild was meeting at John's house, and my palms were sweating and my tongue was thick. The loosely formed organization, without dues or membership cards, had one strict rule: any invited guest could sit in for three meetings, but thereafter, the visitor had to read from his or her work in progress. My time had come.

2 Sara Wright and Sylvester Leeks stood in a corner talking softly. John Clarke was staring at titles in the bookcase. Mary Delaney and Millie Jordan were giving their coats to Grace and exchanging greetings. The other writers were already seated around the living room in a semicircle.

3 John Killens walked past me, touching my shoulder, took his seat and called the meeting to order.

4 "O.K., everybody. Let's start." Chairs scraped the floor and the sounds <u>reverberated</u> in my armpits. "As you know, our newest member, our California singer, is going to read from her new play. What's the title, Maya?"

5 *"One Love. One Life."* My usually deep voiced leaked out high-pitched and weak.

6 A writer asked how many acts the play had. I answered again in the piping voice, "So far only one."

7 Everyone laughed; they thought I was making a joke.

8 "If everyone is ready, we can begin." John picked up his note pad. There was a loud rustling as the writers prepared to take notes.

9 I read the character and set description despite the sudden <u>perversity</u> of my body. The blood pounded in my ears but not enough to drown the skinny sound of my voice. My hands shook so that I had to lay the pages in my lap, but that was not a good solution due to the tricks my knees were playing. They lifted voluntarily, pulling my heels off the floor and then trembled like disturbed Jello. Before I launched into the play's action, I looked around at the writers expecting but hoping not to see their amusement at my predicament. Their faces were <u>studiously</u> blank. Within a year, I was to learn that each had a horror story about a first reading at the Harlem Writers Guild.

10 Time wrapped itself around every word, slowing me. I couldn't force myself to read faster. The pages seemed to be multiplying even as I was trying to reduce them. The play was dull, the characters, unreal, and the dialogue was taken entirely off the back of a Campbell's soup can. I knew this was my first and last time at the Guild. Even if I hadn't the grace to withdraw voluntarily, I was certain the members had a method of separating

68

the wheat from the chaff.

11 "The End." At last.

12 The members laid their notes down beside their chairs and a few got up to use the toilets. No one spoke. Even as I read I knew the drama was bad, but maybe someone would have lied a little.

13 The room filled. Only the whispering of papers shifting told me that the jury was ready.

14 John Henrik Clarke, a <u>taut</u> little man from the South, cleared his throat. If he was to be the first critic, I knew I would receive the worst sentence. John Clarke was famous in the group for his <u>keen</u> intelligence and bitter wit. He had supposedly once told the FBI that they were wrong to think that he would sell out his home state of Georgia; he added that he would give it away, and if he found no takers he would even pay someone to take it.

15 "One Life. One Love?" His voice was a <u>rasp</u> of disbelief. "I found no life and very little love in the play from the opening of the act to its unfortunate end."

16 Using superhuman power, I kept my mouth closed and my eyes on my yellow pad.

17 He continued, his voice lifting. "In 1879, on a March evening, Alexander Graham Bell successfully completed his attempts to send the human voice through a little wire. The following morning some frustrated playwright, unwilling to build the necessary construction plot, began his play with a phone call."

18 A general <u>deprecating</u> murmur floated in the air.

19 "Aw, John" and "Don't be so mean" and "Ooo Johnnn, you ought to be ashamed." Their moans were <u>facetious</u>, mere accompaniment to their <u>relish</u>.

20 Grace invited everyone to drinks, and the crowd rose and started <u>milling</u> around, while I stayed in my chair.

> Angelou discovers that to become a writer, she must learn to put up with stinging criticism.

21 Grace called to me. "Come on, Maya. Have a drink. You need it." I grinned and knew movement was out of the question.

22 Killens came over. "Good thing you stayed. You got some very important criticism." He, too, could slide to hell straddling a knotted greasy rope. "Don't just sit there. If they think you're too sensitive, you won't get such valuable criticism the next time you read."

23 The next time? He wasn't as bright as he looked. I would never see those snooty bastards as long as I stayed black and their asses pointed toward the ground. I put on a nasty-sweet smile on my face and nodded.

24 "That's right, Maya Angelou, show them you can take anything they can dish out. Let me tell you something." He started to sit down beside me, but mercifully another writer called him away.

25 I measured the steps from my chair to the door. I could make it in ten strides.

26 "Maya, you've got a story to tell."

27 I looked up into John Clarke's solemn face.

28 "I think I can speak for the Harlem Writers Guild. We're glad to have you. John Killens came back from California talking about your talent. Well, in this group we remind each other that talent is not enough. You've got to work. Write each sentence over and over again, until it seems you've used every combination possible, then write it again. Publishers don't care much for white writers." He coughed or laughed. "You can imagine what they think about black ones. Come on. Let's get a drink."

Starting Time	
Reading Time	
Finishing Time	
Reading Rate	

∎

COMPREHENSION —

Read the following questions and statements. For each one, put an X in the box before the option that contains the most complete or accurate answer.

1. Angelou's play was called
   □ a. *Living and Loving.*
   □ b. *Today Love, Tomorrow Despair.*
   □ c. *Love Not Today.*
   □ d. *One Love. One Life.*

2. According to John Clarke, being a talented writer was not enough; to succeed, an author must also show
   □ a. humor.
   □ b. perseverance.
   □ c. sensitivity.
   □ d. reverence.

3. The writer develops her ideas through
   □ a. spatial description.
   □ b. comparison.
   □ c. order of importance.
   □ d. time order.

4. The main point of this selection is to tell us how
   □ a. Maya Angelou was accepted into the Harlem Writers Guild.
   □ b. writers form and conduct critique sessions.
   □ c. the Harlem Writers Guild selected new members.
   □ d. Harlem writers went about getting their work published.

5. The selection hints that the head of the Harlem Writers Guild was
   □ a. Maya Angelou.
   □ b. John Henrik Clarke.
   □ c. John Killens.
   □ d. Sarah Wright.

6. In your judgment, which of the following statements is true?
   □ a. Sylvester Leeks was a soft-spoken man.
   □ b. Angelou had good reasons to be nervous about reading her play.
   □ c. John Killens was extremely self-confident.
   □ d. Writers groups offer little support to their members.

7. From this passage we can infer that John Clarke
   □ a. once had an unhappy marriage.
   □ b. was always in trouble with the law.
   □ c. founded the Harlem Writers Guild.
   □ d. disliked his home state of Georgia.

8. The selection ends on a note of
   □ a. hope for Angelou's writing.
   □ b. humor mixed with joy.
   □ c. defeat over Angelou's performance.
   □ d. revenge for black writers.

9. John Clarke's personality may best be described as
   □ a. agreeable.
   □ b. difficult.
   □ c. humorous.
   □ d. sensitive.

10. This selection can be called a complete story because it
    □ a. teaches a moral lesson.
    □ b. relates personal experiences.
    □ c. has a beginning, a middle, and an end.
    □ d. follows all the rules of grammar.

Comprehension Skills
1. recalling specific facts
2. retaining concepts
3. organizing facts
4. understanding the main idea
5. drawing a conclusion
6. making a judgment
7. making an inference
8. recognizing tone
9. understanding characters
10. appreciating literary forms

VOCABULARY, PART TWO —

Write the term that makes the most sense in each sentence.

deprecating   **reverberated**
studiously   **taut**
rasp

1. Angelou's face was _____ with anxiety as she began reading her play.

2. Her voice didn't sound right; it had more of a scratchy _____ than it normally did.

70

3. Her words _____ off the walls of the meeting room.

4. The people in the room listened _____ as she read.

5. She could stand it if they made _____ comments, but compliments would certainly be easier to take.

perversity	milling
facetious	relish
keen	

6. The fact that people avoided her glance showed they did not greet her play with _____.

7. One of the audience offered _____ criticism that cut her like a knife.

8. Perhaps he meant to be somewhat _____, but she did not find his remarks funny at all.

9. What _____ in a man's personality could make him expect someone to laugh at biting criticism?

10. Maya wanted to bury herself in the _____ crowd and be lost to her critics.

Comprehension Score [   ]

Vocabulary Score [   ]

WRITING —

Were you surprised at John Clarke's reaction at the end of the story? Do you think what he says at this point justifies his earlier treatment of Maya? Write a few paragraphs explaining why you think as you do. Use examples from the selection to support your ideas.

STUDY SKILLS —

Read the following passage and answer the questions that follow it.

Specialized Word Lists, I

The two prime sources of words for your specialized lists are your instructors and your textbooks.

Listen during class lectures for the words the speaker repeats and emphasizes. These are likely candidates. Identifying key words will present no problem because experienced lecturers understand the limitations of their listeners. They know that major points need the emphasis of repeated exposure. What would be in bold print in a textbook must be conveyed to students verbally. Be alert to certain words that are stressed and repeated. These are considered important by the lecturer. Especially important terms are often written on the blackboard.

Listen to questions asked that the lecturer answers. Oral quizzing is often used to draw greater attention to important points under discussion.

Another clue to identifying important words and ideas may be found in the length of time devoted to discussion of a single topic. Important points deserve more time.

When you discover that a major term is being presented, try to record the exact definition or explanation given. Being a specialist, your instructor will use precise terminology when defining a concept. Be sure to capture new words exactly as they are used. Indicate with an asterisk or star in your notes that here is a word for your specialized list.

1. Two prime sources for specialized vocabulary lists are your _____ and your textbooks.

2. Experienced instructors make it easy to _____ key words.

3. Important words are stressed, _____ and are often written on the board.

71

4. Because he or she is a specialist, the instructor will use _____ terminology when defining a concept.

5. To help you understand that the group is responding disapprovingly to John Clarke's criticism of Angelou, in paragraphs 18 and 19, an instructor would make sure you knew the meaning of _____.

13 Anticipation

Mabel Dove-Danquah

AUTHOR NOTES—
Mabel Dove-Danquah was born in Ghana, in Africa, and was the first woman to be elected to that country's legislature. She traveled around the world, studying in England and touring in the United States. For a time she was editor of a newspaper in Ghana's capital city, the *Accra Evening News*; later she devoted herself to freelance writing.

Dove-Danquah's short story, "Anticipation," was published in 1960 as part of the collection, *An African Treasury*, which was edited by Langston Hughes.

VOCABULARY, PART ONE—
All of these terms are in the story you are about to read. Study each term and its meaning. Then answer the questions below.

As you read the story, notice how each term is used. You will have more questions about the terms later.

accession, attainment of power

gusto, relish; great enthusiasm

imbibed, drank

attire, apparel; clothing; costume

resplendent, dazzling; stunning

plaited, braided

dotage, weak-minded old age

cynics, sarcastic, untrusting individuals

bland, flat; dull

reclined, leaned back

1. Which general term could be used to name the jeans and T-shirt your friend is wearing? _____

2. Which term could describe the feelings of a person who ate and danced enthusiastically at a party? _____

3. Which term could describe what a person did when he or she consumed liquids?

   _____

4. Which term might describe a meal with little seasoning and no spicy food?

   _____

5. Which term could name people who always think their friends have hidden motives for what they do? _____

A READING PURPOSE—

In this selection a ruler seeks a woman that he thinks he cannot do without. Read to find out how accurate his judgment is.

■

1   Nana Adaku II, Omanhene of Akwasin, was celebrating the twentieth anniversary of his <u>accession</u> to the stool of Akwasin. The capital, Nkwabi, was thronged with people from the outlying towns and villages.

2   It was in the height of the cocoa season, money was circulating freely and farmers were spending to their hearts' content. Friends who had not seen one another for a long time were renewing their friendship. They called with gifts of gin, champagne or whiskey, recalled old days with <u>gusto</u> and before departing <u>imbibed</u> most of the drinks they brought as gifts. No one cared, everyone was happy. Few could be seen in European <u>attire</u>: nearly all were in Gold Coast costume. The men had tokota sandals on their feet, and rich multi-colored velvet and gorgeous, hand-woven kente cloths nicely wrapped round their bodies. The women, with golden ear-rings dangling, with golden chains and bracelets, looked dignified in their colorful native attire.

3   The state drums were beating paeans of joy.

4   It was four o'clock in the afternoon and people were walking to the state park where the Odwira was to be staged. Enclosures of palm leaves decorated the grounds.

5   The Omanhene arrived in a palanquin under a brightly-patterned state umbrella, golden crown on his head, his kente studded with tiny golden beads, rows upon rows of golden necklaces piled high on his chest. He wore bracelets of gold from the wrists right up to the elbows. He held in his right hand a decorated elephant tail which he waved to his enthusiastic, cheering people. In front of him sat his "soul," a young boy of twelve, holding the sword of office.

6   After the Omanhene came the Adontehene, the next in importance. He was <u>resplendent</u> in rich green and red velvet cloth; his head band was studded with golden bars. Other chiefs came one after the other under their brightly-colored state umbrellas. The procession was long. The crowd raised cheers as each palanquin was lowered, and the drums went on beating resounding joys of jubilation. The Omanhene took his seat on the dais with his Elders. The District Commissioner, Captain Hobbs, was near him. Sasa, the jester, looked ludicrous in his motley pair of trousers and his cap of monkey skin. He made faces at the Omanhene, he leered, did acrobatic stunts; the Omanhene could not laugh; it was against custom for the great Chief to be moved to laughter in public.

7   The state park presented a scene of barbaric splendor. Chiefs and their retinue sat on native stools under state umbrellas of diverse colors. The golden

74

linguist staves of office gleamed in the sunlight. The women, like tropical butterflies, looked charming in their multi-colored brocaded silk, kente and velvet, and the Oduku headdress,

> The old chief, bored with his 40 wives, perked up when a new beauty danced into view. To have her he would pay any price.

black and shiny, studded with long golden pins and slides. Young men paraded the grounds, their flowing cloths trailing behind them, their silken plaited headbands glittering in the sun.

8   The drums beat on...

9   The women are going to perform the celebrated Adowa dance. The decorated calabashes make rhythm. The women run a few steps, move slowly sideways and sway their shoulders. One dancer looks particularly enchanting in her green, blue and red square kente, moving with the simple, charming grace of a wild woodland creature; the Chief is stirred, and throws a handful of loose cash into the crowd of dancers. She smiles as the coins fall on her and tinkle to the ground. There is a rush. She makes no sign but keeps on dancing.

10 The Omanhene turns to his trusted linguist:

11 "Who is that beautiful dancer?"

12 "I am sorry, I do not know her."

13 "I must have her as a wife."

14 Nana Adaku II was fifty-five and he had already forty wives, but a new beauty gave him the same new thrill as it did the man who is blessed—or cursed—with only one better half. Desire again burned fiercely in his veins; he was bored with his forty wives. He usually got so mixed up among them that lately he kept calling them by the wrong names. His new wife cried bitterly when he called her Oda, the name of an old, ugly wife.

15 "This dancer is totally different," thought the Chief; "she will be a joy to the palace." He turned round to the linguist:

16 "I will pay one hundred pounds for her."

17 "She might already be married, Nana."

18 "I shall pay the husband any moneys he demands."

19 The linguist knew his Omanhene: when he desired a woman he usually had his way.

20 "Get fifty pounds from the chief treasurer, find the relatives, give them the money and when she is in my palace tonight I shall give her the balance of the fifty pounds. Give the linguist staff to Kojo and begin your investigations now."

21 Nana Adaku II was a fast worker. He was like men all over the world when they are stirred by feminine charm: a shapely leg, the flash of an eye, the quiver of a nostril, the timbre of a voice, and the male species becomes frenzy personified. Many men go through this sort of mania until they reach their dotage. The cynics among them treat women with a little flattery, bland tolerance, and take fine care not to become seriously entangled for life. Women, on the other hand, use quite a lot of common sense: they are not particularly thrilled by the physical charms of a man; if his pockets are heavy and his income sure, he is a good matrimonial risk. But there is evolving a new type of hardheaded modern woman who insists on the perfect lover as well as an income and other necessaries, or stays forever from the unbliss of marriage.

22 By 6 P.M. Nana Adaku II was getting bored with the whole assembly and very glad to get into his palanquin. The state umbrellas danced, the chiefs sat again in their palanquins, the crowd cheered wildly, the drums beat. Soon the shadows of evening fell and the enclosures of palm leaves in the state park stood empty and deserted.

23 The Omanhene had taken his bath after dusk and changed into a gold and green brocaded cloth. Two male servants stood on either side and fanned him with large ostrich feathers as he reclined on a velvet-cushioned settee in his private sitting room. An envelope containing fifty golden sovereigns was near him. He knew his linguist as a man of tact and diplomacy and he was sure that night would bring a wife to help him celebrate the anniversary of his accession to the Akwasin Stool.

24 He must have dozed. When he woke up the young woman was kneeling by his feet. He raised her onto the settee.

25 "Were you pleased to come?"

26 "I was pleased to do Nana's bidding."

27 "Good girl. What is your name?"

28 "Effua, my lord and master."

29 "It is a beautiful name, and you are a beautiful woman too. Here are fifty gold sovereigns, the balance of the marriage dowry. We will marry privately tonight and do the necessary custom afterward." Nana Adaku II is not the first man to use this technique. Civilized, semicivilized and primitive men all over the world have said the very same thing in nearly the same words.

30 "I shall give the money to my mother," said the sensible girl. "She is in the corridor. May I?" The Chief nodded assent.

75

31 Effua returned.

32 "Nana, my mother and other relatives want to thank you for the hundred pounds."

33 "There is no need, my beauty," and he played with the ivory beads lying so snugly on her bosom.

34 "They think you must have noticed some extraordinary charm in me for you to have spent so much money," she smiled shyly at the Omanhene.

35 "But, my dear, you are charming. Haven't they eyes?"

36 "But, Nana, I cannot understand it myself."

37 "You cannot, you modest woman. Look at yourself in that long mirror over there."

38 The girl smiled mischievously, went to the mirror, looked at herself. She came back and sat on the settee and leaned her head on his bosom.

39 "You are a lovely girl, Effua." He caressed her shiny black hair, so artistically plaited.

40 "But, my master, I have always been like this, haven't I?"

41 "I suppose so, beautiful, but I only saw you today."

42 "You only saw me today?"

43 "Today."

44 "Have you forgotten?"

45 "Forgotten what, my love?"

46 "You paid fifty pounds...and married me two years ago."

Starting Time	
Reading Time	
Finishing Time	
■ Reading Rate	

C O M P R E H E N S I O N —

Read the following questions and statements. For each one, put an X in the box before the option that contains the most complete or accurate answer.

1. Nana Adaku II had been on the throne for
   - ☐ a. 5 years.
   - ☐ b. 10 years.
   - ☐ c. 15 years.
   - ☐ d. 20 years.

2. At his stage in life, the Omanhene of Akwasin felt
   - ☐ a. bored.
   - ☐ b. bewildered.
   - ☐ c. content.
   - ☐ d. proud.

3. The facts in this story are presented
   - ☐ a. over a period of a week.
   - ☐ b. within a three-hour time span.
   - ☐ c. throughout a lifetime.
   - ☐ d. as future happenings.

4. If the surprise ending is disregarded, which saying below best suits the selection?
   - ☐ a. Neither a borrower nor a lender be.
   - ☐ b. All that glitters is not gold.
   - ☐ c. Charity begins at home.
   - ☐ d. The grass is always greener on the other side of the fence.

5. We can guess that the story takes place in
   - ☐ a. Africa.
   - ☐ b. Asia.
   - ☐ c. Europe.
   - ☐ d. Australia.

6. The author suggests that women are somewhat
   - ☐ a. sensitive.
   - ☐ b. emotional
   - ☐ c. calculating.
   - ☐ d. creative.

7. Effua's very first reaction to the Omanhene was one of
   - ☐ a. disgust.
   - ☐ b. pity.
   - ☐ c. hysteria.
   - ☐ d. indifference.

8. The author's tone is
   - ☐ a. one that teaches a lesson.
   - ☐ b. light and somewhat humorous.
   - ☐ c. serious and rather scholarly.
   - ☐ d. nostalgic.

9. Nana Adaku II liked to be
   - ☐ a. independent.
   - ☐ b. humble.
   - ☐ c. indulged.
   - ☐ d. appreciated.
10. The selection is written in the form of
    - ☐ a. a court drama.
    - ☐ b. a narrative description.
    - ☐ c. an informal biography.
    - ☐ d. an ancient folk tale.

Comprehension Skills

1. recalling specific facts
2. retaining concepts
3. organizing facts
4. understanding the main idea
5. drawing a conclusion
6. making a judgment
7. making an inference
8. recognizing tone
9. understanding characters
10. appreciating literary forms

VOCABULARY, PART TWO —

Write the term that makes the most sense in each sentence.

accession	**gusto**
attire	**resplendent**
dotage	

1. The _____ clothing of the Omanhene dazzled all the onlookers.

2. To wear brilliant _____ such as this marked him as a very important person.

3. The Omanhene had ruled his land since his _____ to the throne 20 years earlier.

4. The people were enthusiastic about their leader and celebrated with great _____.

5. Even foolish old men in their _____ could not have ignored the celebration.

imbibed	**plaited**
cynics	**bland**
reclined	

6. The Omanhene _____ casually on his throne and watched the performances.

7. The _____ headbands of the dancers resembled the braids in their hair.

8. The Omanhene feasted on delicacies and _____ great quantities of liquor.

9. Only a few _____ would have dared to say that the Omanhene looked bored.

10. The _____ expression on his face gave away his lack of interest.

Comprehension Score [ ]

Vocabulary Score [ ]

WRITING —

What do you think Effua thought of the Omanhene? Write a paragraph that explains your ideas.

STUDY SKILLS —

Read the following passage and answer the questions that follow it.

Specialized Word Lists, II

In addition to instructors, textbooks are a good source of specialized terms. Alert readers soon discover that a chapter frequently hinges on five or six major concepts. Often there are key words associated with these concepts; these are the words to collect and learn.

Such words are often highlighted in bold print or included in headings. If you need additional assurance, refer to questions or other types of summaries that frequently appear at the end of the chapter. These summaries will emphasize major points, the ones the writer wants you to understand and remember.

When you have located the important terms for the unit you are studying, write them down with accompanying definitions and explanations. As you read through the chapter, try to understand these new words and the concepts they represent as fully as you can. If you are not satisfied that your understanding is complete after the first reading, reread parts of the chapter.

Frequently the words you list will be the same ones that are emphasized in class. When this is the case, the instructor will often explain the new terms in words different from those in the text. Be alert to catch these variances because they enrich the meaning of an idea, often increasing its significance for you and making it easier to understand.

A bonus aspect of having studied and learned a term *before* class is that the speaker's remarks will make more sense to you. You will also find that your mind will wander less because of the greater interest and understanding that advance knowledge fosters.

1. Key words associated with _____ concepts are the words to learn.

2. Questions and other types of _____ at the end of the chapter emphasize important points.

3. Write down important terms with accompanying _____ and explanations.

4. Instructors often add to the meaning of a word defined in the text and thereby _____ its significance.

5. For example, with "Anticipation" they might explain that the term _____ means "something added" as well as "attainment of power."

14 | Bloods

Wallace Terry

AUTHOR NOTES—
Wallace Terry was born in New York City, educated at Brown University, The University of Chicago, and Harvard University, and ordained in the Disciples of Christ ministry. He has produced documentary films on black marines and served as a race relations consultant to General David C. Jones when Jones was commanding general of the United States Air Force in Europe. Terry has also been a radio and television commentator for various programs and has written for *USA Today*. In 1983 he was named to the Veterans Administration Advisory Committee on Readjustment Problems of Vietnam Veterans.

Bloods, published in 1984, is a collection of stories told by prisoners of war about their experiences when they were held by the North Vietnamese.

VOCABULARY, PART ONE—
All of these terms are in the story you are about to read. Study each term and its meaning. Then answer the questions below.

As you read the story, notice how each term is used. You will have more questions about the terms later.

evade, to elude; to purposely avoid a situation

conform, to adjust; to be in agreement with

orientation, meetings or sessions to get a person adjusted to new surroundings

crucial, critical; very significant

saturate, to fill to capacity

machete, a large, heavy knife for cutting brush

utilizing, using

stimulated, refreshed; increased the function of

distinctly, unmistakably clearly

medevac, medical evacuation helicopter or ambulance

1. Which term describes what you do if you try to go along with the rules of a group?

   _____

2. Which term could describe a decision that is of great importance in a person's life?

   _____

3. Which term tells what you do if you try to steer clear of something?

   _____

4. Which term describes what you do to grass if you water it so much that the ground can't hold any more water? _____

5. Which term names a vehicle in which you might expect to find a nurse?

   _____

A READING PURPOSE—

This selection shows how a soldier's attitudes changed during his time fighting in Vietnam. As you read, look for the events and occurrences that made him change.

■

1   I really didn't have an opinion of the war at first. I was praying that the war would bypass me. I chose not to <u>evade</u> the draft but to <u>conform</u> to it. I figured it was better to spend two years in the service than five years in prison. And I figured that for nineteen years I had enjoyed a whole lot of fruits of this society. I knew that you don't get anything free in this world.

2   I first arrived in Chu Lai in July 1969. After a week of <u>orientation</u>, I was assigned to the Americal Division, Alpha Company, 1st of the 96th. My company commander was a very good company commander, because he knew his profession and kept us out of a whole lot of <u>crucial</u> incidents. But the second lieutenant—the platoon leader—he was dumb, because he would volunteer us for all kinds of shit details to get brownie points. We would walk point two or three times a week for the whole company. He was literally the word "stupid," because he couldn't read a map. And he would say, "You don't tell me what to do, because they sent me to officers' training school." When we got one or two sniper fire, he would stop right there and call in artillery to <u>saturate</u> the whole area before you could take another step.

3   One time we had to check out an area. It was during the monsoon season. It rained 15 days and 15 nights continuously. We stayed wet 15 days. We started catching cramps and charley horses. And guys' feet got messed up. Well, they were trying to get supplies in to us. But it was raining so hard, the chopper couldn't get in. After five days, we ran out of supplies. We were so hungry and tired we avoided all contact. We knew where the North Vietnamese were, but we knew that if we got into it, they would probably have wiped a big portion of the company out. We were really dropped there to find the North Vietnamese, and here we was hiding from them. Running because we were hungry. We were so far up in the hills that the place was so thick you didn't have to pull guard at night. You'd have to take a <u>machete</u> to cut even 100 meters. It could take two hours, that's how thick the shit was. We starved for four days. That was the first time I was ever introduced to hunger.

4   Then we found some kind of path road down into a little village. And we came to a house that had chickens and stuff there. I think the people abandoned it when they saw us coming. I was the machine gunner, so I had to stay where I was and watch the open area while the guys searched the house. They were city guys who didn't know about <u>utilizing</u> the forest or what they were running into. So they started throwing the rice on the ground. They didn't have the experience that I had. When I was younger, I used to go out for

80

miles of distance into the woods and run the snakes. I told my friend Joe to pick up the rice and get the chickens. So Joe got the stuff. I told them not to worry, so I

> A soldier recalls his service in the jungles of Vietnam and how he made his life-saving decision to get out.

skinned a chicken. I got a whole mess of heat tabs, and put the chicken in my canteen cup and boiled it for a long time. When I thought the chicken was half done, I put in the rice. And a little salt. It was about the only food we had until the bird came in two days after that. Those guys were totally ignorant. They kept calling rice gook food. That's why they threw it on the ground. I told Joe food is food.

5 It was a good thing that I didn't run in the house. Because I saw something about an eighth of a mile away. It looked like a little scarecrow out there in the rice paddy. It was sort of like a little sign. I looked at it real hard. I stretched my eye to make sure it wasn't nobody. Then I seen another little dark object, and it was moving. So I opened my fire immediately. I think the Viet Cong was trying to get around behind us so he could ambush us. I just happened to recognize him. I cut off maybe 50 rounds, and the CO hollered, "Hold up there, Charles. Don't just burn the gun up." The rest of the company told me I really got him, so that was the only person that I really was told I actually killed.

6 My feet was all scriggled up. My skin was raw and coming off. I still carry an infection on my feet right now that I have to visit the VA hospital on a regular basis to take treatment for.

7 Then I started to take drugs to stop the pain in my feet.

8 When one of our men was killed the next day, it didn't make a whole lot of difference, because I just felt good that it wasn't me. But it gave me a thrill like you take a drink of alcohol or smoke a cigarette to see a Viet Cong laying dead. It was giving me a good feeling. It stimulated my senses. I thought about it, and I really started to love seeing someone dead. And I started doing more drugs. Now I'm afraid that if someone catches me the wrong way, I would do them really bodily harm. It won't be no fight to prove who the best man is, or to prove manhood. Because of 'Nam, I cannot fight, because if I fight now, I'll fight for life. Someone is gonna die immediately.

9 But it hurt me bad when they got Joe. Joe was an all right guy from Georgia. I don't know his last name. He talked with that "ol' dude" accent. If you were to see him the first time, you would just say that's a redneck, ridge-runnin' cracker. But he was the nicest guy in the world. We used to pitch our tents together. I would give him food. He would share his water. And food and water was more valuable then than paper money. And when we had an opportunity to stand down, he would get sort of drunk and go around the brothers and say, "Hi there, brother man." The brothers would automatically take offense, but I always told them Joe was all right. His accent was just personal.

10 I remember one night I put my little transistor radio on my pack. We listened to music with the earphones, and he talked about his wife and kids back home on the farm in Georgia. He said he would be glad to see his wife.

11 The next day he was walking point. I was walking the third man behind him when he hit a booby trap. I think it was a 104 round. It blew him up in the air about 8 feet. He came down, and about an inch of flesh was holding his leg to his body. He rested on his buttocks, and his arms were behind him. He was moaning and crying in agony and pain and stuff. What really got to his mind is when he rose himself up and saw his leg blown completely off except that inch. He said, "Oh no, not my legs." I really distinctly remember the look on his face. Then he sort of went into semiconsciousness. He died on the way to the hospital. I had to walk up the trail to guard for medevac to pick him up. And I remember praying to the Lord to let me see some VC—anybody—jump out on that trail.

12 After six months, it was approaching Christmas, and we went back through the jungles to the rear area for a stand-down. That was when I made up in my mind that I wasn't going back to the field. The officers were dumb, but besides that, before I went to Vietnam, I had three dreams that showed me places in Vietnam. When we were in this one area, it was just like in the first dream. I felt like I had been there before, but I didn't place much value on it. But when I seen the second place, it dawned on me this was the place in the second dream. I said that in my dream, there's suppose to be a foxhole approximately 15 feet to the left and a little tin can sittin' on it. At the LZ I was in at the time, I walked straight to the place where the foxhole was suppose to be. And there it was. And the can, too. The third dream said that I was going to be crossing a rice

paddy, and I was going to get shot in my chest with a sucking wound that I would never recover from. And one of my buddies was holding me in his arms, saying I would be all right until the medevac came in. But it seemed like I never made it out of there. So I wrote my mother and told her that it was time to leave the field, or I would never make it out alive. The first and second dreams came true. It was a sign from the Heavenly Father for me to do something, or the third dream would come true. A

Christian never walks into any danger, dumb and blind. Never.

Starting Time [ ]

Reading Time [ ]

Finishing Time [ ]

■ Reading Rate [ ]

COMPREHENSION —

Read the following questions and statements. For each one, put an X in the box before the option that contains the most complete or accurate answer.

1. Joe came from
   - ☐ a. Georgia.
   - ☐ b. Virginia.
   - ☐ c. Mississippi.
   - ☐ d. South Carolina.

2. The narrator leads us to believe that some officers were
   - ☐ a. amusing.
   - ☐ b. friendly.
   - ☐ c. wealthy.
   - ☐ d. incompetent.

3. The narrator presents details according to
   - ☐ a. contrast.
   - ☐ b. spatial order.
   - ☐ c. cause and effect.
   - ☐ d. time order.

4. Choose the best title for this selection.
   - ☐ a. Facts About Vietnam
   - ☐ b. A Decision Based on Experience
   - ☐ c. A Soldier's Last Will
   - ☐ d. Life in a Monsoon Climate

5. How old was the narrator of this article when he entered the service?
   - ☐ a. 17
   - ☐ b. 18
   - ☐ c. 19
   - ☐ d. 20

6. We can make the judgment that the soldiers in this article
   - ☐ a. were not well equipped to face Vietnam's rainy season.
   - ☐ b. tried to overthrow their commanding officer.
   - ☐ c. were all graduates of a military academy.
   - ☐ d. had been properly trained in jungle survival.

7. We can infer that a machine gunner acts as a type of
   - ☐ a. medic.
   - ☐ b. scout.
   - ☐ c. clerk.
   - ☐ d. guard.

8. The last paragraph of this article leaves the reader with a feeling of
   - ☐ a. resignation.
   - ☐ b. enthusiasm.
   - ☐ c. pride.
   - ☐ d. finality.

9. The company commander in this selection can best be described as
   - ☐ a. knowledgeable.
   - ☐ b. unwise.
   - ☐ c. agreeable.
   - ☐ d. jovial.

10. The one-word sentence at the end of this passage is used as a point of
    - ☐ a. humor.
    - ☐ b. emphasis.
    - ☐ c. description.
    - ☐ d. information.

Comprehension Skills

1. recalling specific facts
2. retaining concepts
3. organizing facts
4. understanding the main idea
5. drawing a conclusion
6. making a judgment
7. making an inference
8. recognizing tone

9. understanding characters
10. appreciating literary forms

VOCABULARY, PART TWO —
Write the word that makes the most sense in each sentence.

conform   **orientation**
saturate   **machete**
utilizing

1. By making soup with the chicken and rice, the narrator was _____ materials he found around him.

2. A(n) _____ was given to the soldiers to explain some of the conditions they would face, but it certainly didn't tell them everything.

3. No longer could the soldiers make up their own minds about things; they had to _____ to army rules and regulations.

4. They had to learn to cut paths through the underbrush using a _____.

5. Some felt that their officers were trying to _____ their minds with overwhelming amounts of detail.

evade   **crucial**
stimulated   **distinctly**
medevac

6. The narrator _____ recalled when his friend Joe was hit; the memory of it was burned in his brain.

7. Because he did not see the booby trap he stepped on, there was no way for him to _____ it.

8. If Joe was to live, getting medical attention immediately was _____.

9. They could only hope that the _____ to take him away would come quickly.

10. The incident _____ the narrator's emotions, making him feel passionately that he had to get home.

Comprehension Score [   ]

Vocabulary Score [   ]

WRITING —
Over the course of this selection the narrator's attitude about wanting to be in Vietnam changes. Write a few paragraphs explaining what causes this change. Include at least three things that happened to cause it.

STUDY SKILLS —
Read the following passage and answer the questions that follow it.

Using Specialized Lists
You will naturally want your lists of specialized terms to be readily accessible and easy to use when you need them. There are different ways to accomplish this.

Some students list each word on its own 3×5 card along with the definition and an explanation. The cards can be filed alphabetically or by unit. Words recorded in this fashion are easily sorted, located, and reviewed.

Others prefer to use their notebooks. This arrangement allows new terms to be recorded close to the notes accompanying the lecture or chapter where the new terms were first used. Words catalogued this way make reviewing easier since you are able to use your knowledge of the terms as an aid to recall important concepts from the lecture or text.

Each night new terms should be studied during the review and memorization segment of your study period. The words will then be fresh in your mind for class the following day.

Periodically (before midterm examinations, for example), all specialized terms should be reviewed and studied. It is prudent at this time to attempt to write the definition of each term from memory. It is important to recall the exact wording since precise definitions are more useful to you both in understanding the subject matter and in demonstrating your understanding to your instructor.

1. Index cards enable students to file new words _____ or by unit.

2. Words listed in a _____ can be recorded close to the notes from the lecture where the words were first used.

3. New terms should be _____ each night.

4. Periodically the student should attempt to write the definition of each term from _____.

5. Memorization could help you recall that the definition of _____ in the story you just read is "critical; very significant."

84

Showing My Color

Clarence Page

AUTHOR NOTES—
Clarence Page is a Pulitzer Prize-winning journalist and television commentator who deals with African-American as well as many other issues. His regular column, which is syndicated by the *Chicago Tribune*, appears in over 100 American newspapers; he has also written for the *New Republic* and *The Wall Street Journal*. Page frequently offers insightful commentary on such programs as National Public Radio's *Sunday Morning Edition* and PBS's *The MacLaughlin Group*. He presently lives in Maryland.

Showing My Color: Impolite Essays on Race and Identity was published in 1996.

VOCABULARY, PART ONE—

All of these terms are in the story you are about to read. Study each term and its meaning. Then answer the questions below.

As you read the story, notice how each term is used. You will have more questions about the terms later.

prestigious, having a very good reputation; famous

pose, pretense

tandem, close togetherness

daunting, frightening; intimidating

debilitating, exhausting; crippling

derided, made fun of

mediocre, fair; no better than average

dispel, to get rid of; to drive away

affluent, wealthy

bleak, dreary; dismal

1. Which term could describe people who had a great amount of money?

   _____

2. Which term describes something that is not very good but not terribly bad?

   _____

3. Which term would you use in describing a race you ran in that left you completely worn out? _____

4. Which term could describe a college that is considered one of the best in the country? _____

5. For which term is *gloomy* a synonym? _____

A READING PURPOSE—

In this selection Page presents a description of young blacks' attitude toward education.
As you read, decide if you think his opinions are justified.

■

1 It might have been just another shooting of a would-be mugger by his intended victim, who happened to be an undercover police officer. But this young mugger in the summer of 1985 in the Morningside Heights section of Manhattan turned out to be Edmund Perry, who ten days earlier had graduated from Philips Exeter, one of America's most <u>prestigious</u> prep schools, with a scholarship to Stanford in the fall.

2 Thus opened one of the great urban mysteries of the 1980s. Perry, a product of the Harlem ghetto, had been scouted by a program that has given scholarships at eastern prep schools to low-income black youths who show high potential. Most have been heartwarming success stories. Why did this one fail? Most important: What did his fate say about the forces that pull so many others back into the maelstrom of ghetto pathologies? What are the cultural factors that cause so many other black youths, particularly young black males, to shun the opportunities that have opened up to blacks since the 1960s and put on the brakes instead? If racism, even the legacy of slavery, plays a part, what is the part, when young black males kill more young black males every year than the Ku Klux Klan did over several decades?

3 I think an important clue is to be found in their own adolescent values, particularly the quest to be "cool," a mission that occupies ultimate importance in the way most young black males define manhood. In literal translation from black slang, "cool" means "excellent" or "first rate." One speaks of a "cool pair of sneakers" or of hearing "cool jams" at a "cool party." It can also mean self-control, as in "I was cool" in the face of a stressful situation. But on a deeper level, "cool" also describes a pattern of social acceptability and a psychological <u>pose</u> that serves as a coping mechanism for social and psychological survival. In <u>tandem</u> with the <u>daunting</u>, reflexive rejection the larger society imposes on young, poor black males, it describes the pull of the ghetto, a morally <u>debilitating</u> subculture of self-defeating and irresponsible attitudes and behaviors.

4 Two years after Perry died, a study by two anthropologists, Signithia Fordham of the University of the District of Columbia and John U. Ogbu of the University of California, focused national attention on a major damaging factor in this quest for cool: negative peer pressure that <u>derided</u> academic success as "acting white."

5 Although the persecution of nerds is hardly a new development in the cultural life of teenagers, it has taken on a particularly tragic manifestation among poor urban blacks in the post-civil rights era. In a study of an unidentified 99 percent black District of Columbia high school, Fordham spent a year

86

interviewing thirty-three students. She found otherwise promising black youths driven to unusual extremes to avoid visible signs of academic success.

> Is it "trying to act white" or trying to get a good education? Clarence Page thinks students should worry less about the acting-white part.

6   A football player identified as "Sidney" had fallen from his earlier A's and B's to <u>mediocre</u> scores on standardized tests to <u>dispel</u> fears of being called "Mr. Advanced Placement," he told Fordham.

7   "Shelvy," once an honor roll student, also had experienced falling grades to avoid being called a "Brainiac." Most other "Brainiacs" will "sit back and they know the answer and they won't answer it," she told Fordham, "'cause see, first thing everybody say, 'Well, they're trying to show off.'"

8   More recently, a black seventeen-year-old at <u>affluent</u> suburban Bethesda-Chevy Chase High School was quoted in the *Washington Post* as saying he turned down offers of a place in an honors math class despite his high ability because he did not want to be the only black student in the class. "It would have been hard to relate [to white students]. I wouldn't have been able to relax...I would have been alone and isolated. [But] by the end of the year, I thought geometry was pretty easy. I wish I had taken the honors math."

9   Cedric, another stunning example of a black District of Columbia teen with bright ambitions despite his <u>bleak</u> background, came to the attention of the *Wall Street Journal* and ABC's "Nightline" in 1994. His mother was a clerical worker. His father was in the penitentiary. By the early 1990s, his neighborhood near Frank W. Ballou High School had become one of the District of Columbia's war zones. In one school year, a student was shot dead by a classmate, another boy was attacked with an ax, a girl was badly wounded in a knife fight—with another girl—and the body of an unidentified man was discovered early one morning in the school dumpster.

10   Cedric would check in at the school's computer lab every morning, usually before 7:30 A.M., and stay sometimes until dusk, escaping into the electronic community of cyberspace. He was one of only eighty students who can boast an average of B or better at the school, where the total enrollment is 1,350. Yet he was not much honored among his peers, and it was having an effect. Cedric skipped two assemblies at which he was to receive academic honors. He was not alone. Some honorees showed up but refused to stand up until teachers pushed them to the stage. The principal admitted that he had tried to keep the assembly's purpose a secret, because so many honored students had been ridiculed by their peers as "goody" or "nerd," or, worst of all, it seemed, as "trying to act white."

11   "White" has long meant uncool in the language of black youths. In my youth, "actin' white" was a comparatively innocent critique for anyone who didn't walk, talk, dance, or shoot baskets with sufficient style, grace, or grandiosity. "He shoots like a white boy," we might say on the basketball court of anyone who preferred flat-footed long shots to the more daring running, weaving, and dribbling up close to the basket for a magnificent leaping jump shot. But to today's hip-hop generation, "white" has come to mean something far more sinister: the "enemy."

12   One friend of Cedric's told the *Journal* reporter that Cedric's attempts to make it in a white man's world are seen as "a type of disrespect to us."

13   Disrespect? Yes, it is. Ambition shows no respect to those who choose to stay behind. By the 1990s, young black males had become the most feared creatures on America's urban scene. Those who have few other achievements to show in their lives, who have grown up amid poverty and violence and the fear—or reality—of homelessness at any moment, have taken the fear they invoke in the eyes of the straight world—the "white" world—as a badge of honor, a cloak that says, *Yes, at least I am better at something than you are!*

Starting Time [   ]

Reading Time [   ]

Finishing Time [   ]

■ Reading Rate [   ]

COMPREHENSION —

Read the following questions and statements. For each one, put an X in the box before the option that contains the most complete or accurate answer.

1. Edmund Berry had just graduated from
   - ☐ a. Morningside Heights.
   - ☐ b. Chevy Chase.
   - ☐ c. Philips Exeter.
   - ☐ d. Ballou.

2. Page believes that some young black men enjoy being feared because
   - ☐ a. it is one way they can be better than whites.
   - ☐ b. it makes going to school bearable.
   - ☐ c. it is something to brag about to their girlfriends.
   - ☐ d. they see it as a substitute for an education.

3. The organization of the material in this selection is
   - ☐ a. chronological order.
   - ☐ b. an opening anecdote followed by an argument based on it.
   - ☐ c. an opening anecdote followed by a flashback.
   - ☐ d. a series of examples and comments.

4. The message Clarence Page wants to convey in this selection is
   - ☐ a. don't be too cool to get a good education.
   - ☐ b. black students have to have some way of standing out in the crowd.
   - ☐ c. students like Edmund Perry would never have a chance in the white world.
   - ☐ d. boys are less inclined to take education seriously than girls are.

5. Looking at the students mentioned in the selection, the reader might say in fairness that the problem
   - ☐ a. is almost entirely a ghetto issue.
   - ☐ b. hits both rich and poor black males.
   - ☐ c. hits poor black males and females equally.
   - ☐ d. is almost entirely an issue with well-to-do black students.

6. Page feels that black youth today
   - ☐ a. feel the same about whites that his generation did.
   - ☐ b. get along better with whites than his generation did.
   - ☐ c. have more bad feelings about whites than his generation did.
   - ☐ d. would rather go to segregated schools.

7. Fordham and Ogbu did a study of poor-performing black students because
   - ☐ a. they had heard the term *acting white* and wanted to find out what it meant.
   - ☐ b. they saw it as a problem that people needed to pay attention to.
   - ☐ c. their own children were doing badly in high school.
   - ☐ d. they wanted to prove that blacks students were less motivated than whites.

8. Clarence Page's attitude about the students he describes is
   - ☐ a. sympathetic and understanding.
   - ☐ b. angry and threatening.
   - ☐ c. angry but unconcerned.
   - ☐ d. surprised and upset.

9. How did Cedric approach his education?
   - ☐ a. He wanted to do well but was embarrassed to let others know.
   - ☐ b. He wanted to do well and bragged about how smart he was.
   - ☐ c. He tried very hard but couldn't succeed.
   - ☐ d. He did well enough to pass even though he didn't try very hard.

10. When Page uses the expression "He shoots like a white boy," he is using a
   - ☐ a. simile.
   - ☐ b. metaphor.
   - ☐ c. literal comparison.
   - ☐ d. symbol.

Comprehension Skills
1. recalling specific facts
2. retaining concepts
3. organizing facts
4. understanding the main idea
5. drawing a conclusion
6. making a judgment
7. making an inference
8. recognizing tone
9. understanding characters
10. appreciating literary forms

VOCABULARY, PART TWO—
Write the term that makes the most sense in each sentence.

pose   daunting
derided   mediocre
affluent

1. Page believes that many black kids are content to be _____ students rather than good ones.

2. They want to be accepted by their friends, not _____ by them.

3. Page thinks this tough-guy attitude is a _____, that underneath students are really somewhat fearful.

4. He sees the attitude in _____ students as well as in poor ones.

5. It is _____ to stand up alone and not follow the crowd.

prestigious   tandem
debilitating bleak
dispel

6. Page feels that students must _____ their I-don't-need-it attitudes about education.

7. He believes their futures will be _____ and unpromising unless they do.

8. A few students have high hopes and want to get into _____ colleges.

9. These students work extra hard at odd hours, sometimes in _____ with others but usually alone.

10. It can be _____ to work so hard and yet keep your efforts a secret from others.

Comprehension Score [   ]

Vocabulary Score [   ]

WRITING—
Is Clarence Page's article describing anyone you know? Write a paragraph describing a person who has the attitudes Page talks about. Then write a second paragraph that explains why you think the person feels this way and if he or she has good reason for these attitudes.

STUDY SKILLS—
Read the following passage and answer the questions that follow it.

Other Word Study, I

1. Contextual Aids. By seeing a word in context, we come to know it better and better with every exposure. At first, the word becomes part of our reading vocabulary. This means that we have seen it often enough to recognize it and remember its meaning. Many words remain just in our reading vocabulary. Other new words are repeated in print often enough for us to come to know them well; these words are then assimilated into our writing vocabulary. When a word finally becomes totally familiar, it may join our speaking vocabulary.

When read in context, words often have different shades of meaning that are imperceptible when read from a list. A simple word like *root*, for example, has at least 22 different meanings. The word *perception* has very different meanings in law and in psychology. You can't even know how to pronounce *precedent*, let alone know its meaning, without seeing how it is being used. And the only way to avoid confusion between words like *precept* and *percept* is to learn them in context.

Further, relating a word to the way it is used increases our understanding not only of the word but also of the idea the word represents. Consequently, words learned through context are more permanent than those learned from lists.

2. Affixes and Roots. Still another kind of word study centers around prefixes, suffixes, and roots. Because both prefixes and suffixes are added to words, collectively they are called affixes.

1. Every time we see a word in context we get to know it _____.

2. When we know a word completely, it becomes part of our _____ vocabulary.

3. Some _____ of meaning are imperceptible when words are not read in context.

4. For example, the word _____ in this selection means "close togetherness," but in another context it can mean a two-rider bicycle.

5. Prefixes and suffixes are both _____ to words.

16

Let the Trumpet Sound

Stephen B. Oates

AUTHOR NOTES—
A professional biographer, Stephen B. Oates has researched and written biographies of Nat Turner, John Brown, Abraham Lincoln, William Faulkner, Clara Barton, and Martin Luther King, Jr.

In writing *Let the Trumpet Sound,* Oates utilized the Martin Luther King Collection at Boston University, collections at the Martin Luther King, Jr. Center for Nonviolent Social Change in Atlanta, and other public and private sources.

VOCABULARY, PART ONE—
All of these terms are in the story you are about to read. Study each term and its meaning. Then answer the questions below.

As you read the story, notice how each term is used. You will have more questions about the terms later.

phenomenal, extraordinary; sensational

precocious, showing mature qualities at an early age

rollicking, lively

deferential, submissive; obedient

rancid, foul-smelling

decrepit, run-down; shabby

coveted, eagerly desired and held

injunction, instruction; command

demeaned, degraded; lowered

admonished, warned; scolded

1. Which term best describes a child who can read before he or she starts school?

   _____

2. Which term could describe a building with peeling paint and broken windows?

   _____

3. Which term could describe a person who always quietly does what her boss tells her to do? _____

4. Which term could describe one of the qualities of sour milk?

   _____

5. How might a person feel who was embarrassed in front of others?

   _____

A READING PURPOSE —

This selection discusses some of the early experiences of Martin Luther King, Jr.'s, life.
Read it to find some of the key lessons he learned during those years.

■

1   The adults remarked about how intelligent he was, how he could see and feel things beyond the understanding of most children, how he could drive you to distraction with all his questions. When his family rode through Atlanta, he observed all the Negroes standing in breadlines and asked his parents about them. It was the middle of the Depression, and 65 percent of Atlanta's black population was on public relief. M. L. was deeply affected by the sight of those tattered folk, worried lest their children not have enough to eat.

2   Yes, the adults said, he was a brilliant child, a gifted child, who could talk like he was grown sometimes. My, how that boy loved language. "You just wait and see," he once told his parents. "When I grow up I'm going to get me some big words." "Even before he could read," his Daddy boasted, "he kept books around him, he just liked the idea of having them." And his memory was phenomenal. By age five, he could recite whole Biblical passages and sing entire hymns from memory. His parents and grandmother all praised him for his precocious ways, making him flush with self-esteem. In fact, he was so bright that his parents slipped him into grade school a year early. Daddy recalled what happened next. "He was always a talkative chap, you know. So he shot his mouth off and told them he was only five while the other children were six, so they booted him right out of that class."

3   At six, he began signing hymns at church groups and conventions, accompanied by Mother Dear on the piano. Now he belted out a rollicking gospel song, now groaned through a slow and sobbing hymn. He sang his favorite with "a blues fervor." It was " I Want to Be More and More Like Jesus." People often wept and "rocked with joy" when he performed for them. But he "didn't get puffed up," his Daddy related, and sat down quietly when he was finished. Frankly, all the fuss embarrassed him.

4   In his preschool years, M. L.'s closest playmate was a white boy whose father owned a store across the street from the King home. In September, 1935, the two chums entered school—separate schools, M. L. noticed. He attended Younge Street Elementary School with Christine and there was not a single white child there. Then the parents of his friend announced that M. L. could no longer play with their son. But why? he sputtered. "Because we are white and you are colored."

5   Later, around the dinner table, he confided in his parents what had happened, and for the first time they told him about "the race problem." They recounted the history of slavery in America, told how it had ended with Abraham Lincoln and the Civil War, explained how whites eventually maintained their superiority by segregating Negroes and making them feel like slaves every day of their lives. But his mother counseled him, "You must never feel

that you are less than anybody else. You must always feel that you are *somebody*." He did feel that he was somebody. Everyone told him how smart and sensitive he was, praised him for his extraordinary ways. Yes, he had an idea he was somebody.

> Young M. L. had to learn more than he was taught at school. He had to learn the language and customs, the whys and wherefores, of a white society founded on prejudice.

Still, this race trouble was disturbing. "As my parents discussed some of the tragedies that had resulted from this problem and some of the insults they themselves had confronted on account of it, I was greatly shocked, and from that moment on I was determined to hate every white person."

6 So it was that M. L. began his real education in Atlanta, Georgia. Oh, he studied arithmetic, grammar, and history at school, passing easily through the lower grades and transferring in the sixth grade to David T. Howard Colored Elementary School, where he was <u>deferential</u> to teachers, considerate of his peers, precocious and diligent as always. But as with other Negro children, his true education was to learn in countless painful ways what it meant to be black in white America. He found out that he—a preacher's boy—could not buy a Coke or a hamburger at the downtown stores. He could not even sit at the lunch counters there. He had to drink from a "colored" water fountain, relieve himself in a <u>rancid</u> "colored" restroom, and ride a rickety "colored" freight elevator. White drugstores and soda fountains, if they served him at all, made him stand at a side window for ice cream, which came to him in a paper cup. White people, of course, got to eat their ice cream out of dishes. If he rode a city bus, he had to sit in the back as though he were contaminated. If he wanted to see a new movie in a downtown theater, he had to enter through a side door and sit in the "colored section" in the back balcony. Of course, he could always go to the <u>decrepit</u> "colored" movie house, with its old films and faded and fluttering screen.

7 He learned, too, how white Atlantans loved their Confederate heritage, cherished the halcyon days when plantations and slavery flourished in the surrounding countryside. He witnessed all the fanfare that attended the world premiere of the motion picture *Gone With the Wind*, which opened in Atlanta

on December 15, 1939, when he was ten. White Atlanta quivered with excitement when Clark Gable, Olivia de Havilland, Vivien Leigh and her husband Laurence Olivier, all came to town for the opening. There was a gala parade downtown, then a grand ball at the auditorium, festooned with Rebel flags. Here white Atlantans reveled in songs like "Suwanee River," "Carry Me Back to Old Virginny," and "My Old Kentucky Home," and danced waltzes like southerners of old. The next night more than 2,000 white Atlantans crowded into Lowe's Grand Theater to see what they fantasized was the world of their ancestors portrayed in living color, a world of cavalier gentlemen and happy darkies, of elegant ladies and breathless belles in crinoline, a world that was lost forever in the Civil War. With its <u>coveted</u> myths and racial stereotypes (a good "nigger" was a loyal and obsequious slave, a bad "nigger" was an uppity and impudent black who rode in the same buckboard with a Yankee carpetbagger), *Gone With the Wind* became one of the most popular motion pictures ever produced in America, playing to millions of whites all over the land.

8 This too M. L. learned: a good nigger was a black who minded his own business and accepted the way things were without dissent. And so his education went. He discovered that whites referred to Negroes as "boys" and "girls" regardless of age. He saw WHITES ONLY signs staring back at him almost everywhere: in the windows of barber shops and all the good restaurants and hotels, at the YMCA, the city parks, golf courses, and swimming pools, and in the waiting rooms of train and bus stations. He found that there were even white and black sections of Atlanta and that he resided in "nigger town."

9 Segregation caused a tension in the boy, a tension between his mother's <u>injunction</u> (remember, you are *somebody*) and a system that <u>demeaned</u> and insulted him every day, saying, "You are less than, you are not equal to." He struggled with that tension, struggled with the pain and rage he felt when a white woman in a downtown store slapped him and called him "a little nigger"...when he stood on the very spot in Atlanta where whites had lynched a Negro... when he witnessed nightriding Klansmen beat Negroes in the streets there...when he saw "with my own eyes" white cops brutalize Negro children. When his parents <u>admonished</u> him to love whites because it was his Christian duty, M. L. asked defiantly: "How can I love a race of people who hate me?"

10 Besides, he didn't think his Daddy really loved them either. His Daddy stood up to whites, the way Grandfather Williams used to do. Yes, Daddy was always "straightening out the white folks." He would not let white agents make collections at his house. He would not ride the city buses and suffer the humiliation of having to sit in a colored section. He would not let whites call him "boy." One day when M. L. was riding with his Daddy in the family car, a white patrolman pulled him over and snapped, "Boy, show me your license." Daddy shot back, "Do you see this child here?" He pointed at M. L. "That's a *boy* there. I'm a *man*. I'm Reverend King."

11 "When I stand up," King said, "I want everybody to know that a *man* is standing." "Nobody," he asserted, "can make a slave out of you if you don't think like a slave." "I don't care how long I have to live with the system. I am never going to accept it. I'll fight it until I die."

Starting Time	
Reading Time	
Finishing Time	
■ Reading Rate	

COMPREHENSION —

Read the following questions and statements. For each one, put an X in the box before the option that contains the most complete or accurate answer.

1. M. L. lived in
   - ☐ a. New York City.
   - ☐ b. Atlanta.
   - ☐ c. Nashville.
   - ☐ d. Little Rock.

2. The Kings wanted M. L. to forgive the whites because
   - ☐ a. it was the only way to survive.
   - ☐ b. the Kings wanted to be like the whites.
   - ☐ c. the Kings were Christians.
   - ☐ d. not all whites were prejudiced.

3. The details of this article are arranged
   - ☐ a. spatially.
   - ☐ b. in chronological order.
   - ☐ c. as a simple list.
   - ☐ d. in order of importance.

4. Which of the following might be the best title for this selection?
   - ☐ a. The Dawn of Desire
   - ☐ b. Freedom for All
   - ☐ c. A Dream Come True
   - ☐ d. A Rude Awakening

5. We can conclude that the Younge Street Elementary School was
   - ☐ a. not integrated.
   - ☐ b. old and rickety.
   - ☐ c. on the edge of town.
   - ☐ d. for white children only.

6. We can make the judgment that since M. L. was black,
   - ☐ a. he could not wear white clothes.
   - ☐ b. he was not allowed to enter movie theaters.
   - ☐ c. he was not expected to attend school.
   - ☐ d. he could not eat at the restaurant of his choice.

7. This article suggests that
   - ☐ a. Reverend King was a militant leader.
   - ☐ b. M. L.'s view of society was formed at an early age.
   - ☐ c. Mrs. King held an unrealistic view of her station in life.
   - ☐ d. segregation was abolished during the 1930s.

8. In this selection the writer uses tone
   - ☐ a. to highlight attitudes.
   - ☐ b. to express an opinion.
   - ☐ c. to amuse the reader.
   - ☐ d. to show fear.

9. Before he started school, M. L.'s view of the world had been
   - ☐ a. free of bitterness.
   - ☐ b. tainted by race hatred.
   - ☐ c. quite realistic.
   - ☐ d. humorous.

10. In the second paragraph the writer reveals M. L.'s character through the use of
    ☐ a. vivid description.
    ☐ b. figurative language.
    ☐ c. direct quotes.
    ☐ d. shocking exclamations.

Comprehension Skills

1. recalling specific facts
2. retaining concepts
3. organizing facts
4. understanding the main idea
5. drawing a conclusion
6. making a judgment
7. making an inference
8. recognizing tone
9. understanding characters
10. appreciating literary forms

VOCABULARY, PART TWO—

Write the term that makes the most sense in each sentence.

precocious   **rollicking**
decrepit   **demeaned**
admonished

1. Young M. L. could stir up crowds of worshippers with a _____ Gospel song.

2. Because their son was so _____, the Kings enrolled him in school a year early.

3. Unlike the modern schools reserved for whites, his school was run-down and _____.

4. M. L. felt _____ by the unfair treatment he received from many whites.

5. His parents did not approve of his dislike of whites and _____ him to be charitable to everyone.

phenomenal   **deferential**
rancid   **coveted**
injunction

6. M. L. was upset by the _____ difference in life for blacks and whites.

7. Many whites certainly did not follow the _____ "Love thy neighbor as thyself."

8. Their _____ belief, one that they would be willing to die defending, was that they were better than blacks.

9. Blacks were supposed to be humble and _____ to them.

10. They could feast at banquets while blacks ate _____, spoiled food.

Comprehension Score [   ]

Vocabulary Score [   ]

WRITING—

How do you think Martin Luther King, Jr. went from a young person, at one point, "determined to hate every white person" to later being a preacher at the head of a nonviolent movement? Do you see any contradiction between his childhood and adult ideas? Write a few paragraphs explaining what you think and why you think as you do.

STUDY SKILLS—

Read the following passage and answer the questions that follow it.

Other Word Study, II

When a prefix is added to the beginning of a word, it causes a change in the meaning of that word. For example, the prefix un-, when added to a word like happy, gives the word a completely opposite meaning.

Suffixes are added to the ends of words. Although they do not affect the basic meaning of a word, suffixes frequently alter its part of speech. For example, a verb, *hate,* can become an adjective, *hateful,* when a suffix is added.

Word roots are often Latin and Greek stems on which many of our English words are based. *Bio,* which means "life", is a Greek root word. From it we get such English words as *biology* and *antibiotic* etc.

Through the study of affixes and roots, you can get a better feel for the meaning of many new words. Understanding how a word has acquired its particular meaning makes it much more likely that the word will become a part of your vocabulary. Check in a good dictionary each new word you encounter. The origin of the root of the word is usually explained.

As you become more familiar with words—their origins (etymology) and their formative parts—you will find that new and difficult words will be much less daunting when you meet them.

1. A prefix is an affix added to the

   _____ of a word.

2. A suffix is an affix added to the

   _____ of a word.

3. In the selection about Martin Luther King, the affix *-tion* changes the word *education* from a verb, *educate,* to a(n) _____.

4. Word roots are often _____ on words of Greek or Latin origin.

5. To discover the origin of a word, one should consult a good _____.

A Man's Life

Roger Wilkins

AUTHOR NOTES—

Roger Wilkins was born in Kansas City, Missouri, and received his law degree in 1956 from the University of Michigan. He practiced international law in New York City for several years before joining the Agency for International Development in Washington, D.C. From 1966 until 1969, Wilkins served as assistant attorney general with the U.S. Department of Justice. He then directed the Ford Foundation's domestic program until 1972.

A career change led Wilkins to the *Washington Post*, where his editorials on the Watergate scandal helped earn the paper a Pulitzer Prize nomination. He has also been an editorial writer for the *New York Times* and a member of the staff of *Nation*. In 1983–1984 he was senior advisor to Jesse Jackson's presidential campaign. He currently teaches at George Mason University.

VOCABULARY, PART ONE—

All of these terms are in the story you are about to read. Study each term and its meaning. Then answer the questions below.

As you read the story, notice how each term is used. You will have more questions about the terms later.

dispirited, discouraged and saddened

gross, glaring; very easily recognized

symbiotic, association of two unlike things paired together so that each benefits

montage, a picture made up of many smaller pictures; a mixture

excruciatingly, painfully

tangible, capable of being perceived by touch

partisan, strongly supporting a political party or cause

sinister, evil; having bad intentions

aspirations, hopes; desires

frivolous, silly; not to be taken seriously

1. Which term might you use in describing an error that was very obvious?

   _____

2. Which term could describe a person who has stickers for the Republican Party pasted all over his car? _____

3. Which term could describe how shy a child is if she hides behind the couch when company comes? _____

4. Which term could describe the villain in a movie? _____

5. Which term might describe a comedy routine? _____

A READING PURPOSE—

This selection describes an incident that occurred at a banquet in the late 1960s. As you read, decide if the same incident would likely have occurred today.

■

1 When it was all over, a number of men had tears in their eyes, even more had lifted hearts and spirits, but a few were so <u>dispirited</u> that they went upstairs to get drunk. We had just heard the President and Vice-President of the United States in a unique piano duet—and to many old Gridiron Dinner veterans, it was a moving showstopper. To a few others, it was a depressing display of <u>gross</u> insensitivity and both conscious and unconscious racism—further proof that they and their hopes for their country are becoming more and more isolated from those places where America's heart and power seem to be moving.

2 The annual dinner of the Gridiron Club is the time when men can put on white ties and tails and forget the anxiety and loneliness that are central to the human condition and look at other men in white ties and tails and know that they have arrived or are still there.

3 The guests are generally grateful and gracious. But the event's importance is beyond the structures of graciousness because it shows the most powerful elements of the nation's daily press and all elements of the nation's government locked in a <u>symbiotic</u> embrace. The rich and the powerful tell many truths in jest about themselves and about their country. I don't feel very gracious about what they told me.

4 Some weeks ago, to my surprise and delight, a friend—a sensitive man of honor—with a little half-apology about the required costume, invited me to attend the dinner.

5 The first impression was stunning: almost every passing face was a familiar one. Some had names that were household words. Some merely made up a <u>montage</u> of the familiar faces and bearings of our times. There were Richard Helms and Walter Mondale and Henry Kissinger and George McGovern and Joel Broyhill and Tom Wicker and William Westmoreland and John Mitchell and Tom Clark (ironically placed, by some pixie no doubt, next to each other on the dais) and Robert Finch and Ralph Nader and, of course, the President of the United States.

6 One thing quickly became clear about those faces. Apart from Walter Washington—who, I suppose, as Mayor had to be invited—mine was the only face in a crowd of some five hundred that was not white. There were no Indians, there were no Asians, there were no Puerto Ricans, there were no Mexican-Americans. There were just the mayor and me. Incredibly, I sensed that there were few in that room who thought that anything was missing.

7 There is something about an atmosphere like that that is hard to define but <u>excruciatingly</u> easy for a

black man to feel. It is the heavy, almost <u>tangible</u>, clearly visible broad assumption that in places where it counts, America is a white country. I was an American citizen sitting in a banquet

> At a Washington dinner Roger Wilkins discovers a subtle and disturbing racism among the power elite.

room in a hotel that I had visited many times.... This night in that room, less than three miles from my home in the nation's capital, a 60 percent black city, I felt out of place in America.

8 That is not to say that there were not kind men, good men, warm men, in and around and about the party, nor is it to say that anyone was personally rude to me. There were some old friends and some new acquaintances whom I was genuinely glad to see. Ed Muskie, who had given a very funny and exquisitely <u>partisan</u> speech (the Republicans have three problems: the war, inflation, and what to say on Lincoln's Birthday), was one of those. I was even warmly embraced by the Deputy Attorney General, Mr. Kleindienst, and had a long conversation with the associate director of the FBI, Mr. DeLoach.

9 But it was not the people so much who shaped the evening. It was the humor amidst that pervasive whiteness about what was going on in this country these days that gave the evening its form and substance. There were many jokes about the "Southern strategy." White people have funny senses of humor. Some of them found something to laugh about in the Southern strategy. Black people don't think it's funny at all. That strategy hits men where they live—in their hopes for themselves and their dreams for their children. We find it <u>sinister</u> and frightening. And let it not be said that the Gridiron Club and its guests are not discriminating about their humor. There was a real sensitivity about the inappropriateness of poking fun that night about an ailing former President but none about laughing about policies that crush the <u>aspirations</u> of millions of citizens of this nation. An instructive distinction, I thought....

10 As the jokes about the Southern strategy continued, I thought about the one-room segregated schoolhouse where I began my education in Kansas City. That was my neighborhood school. When they closed it, I was bused—without an apparent second

thought—as a five-year-old kindergartner, across town to the black elementary school. It was called Crispus Attucks.

11 And I thought of the day I took my daughter, when she was seven, along the Freedom Trail, in Boston, and of telling her about the black man named Crispus Attucks who was the first American to die in our revolution. And I remember telling her that white America would try very hard in thousands of conscious and unconscious ways both to make her feel that her people had had no part in building America's greatness and to make her feel inferior. And I remember the profoundly moving and grateful look in her eyes and the wordless hug she gave me when I told her, "Don't you believe them because they are lies." And I felt white America in that room in the Statler Hilton telling me all those things that night, and I told myself, "Don't you believe them because they are lies."

12 And when it came to the end, the President and the Vice-President of the United States, in an act which they had consciously worked up, put on a Mr. Bones routine about the Southern strategy with the biggest boffo coming as the Vice-President affected a deep Southern accent. And then they played their duets—the President playing his songs, the Vice-President playing "Dixie," the whole thing climaxed by "God Bless America" and "Auld Lang Syne." The crowd ate it up. They roared. As they roared I thought that after our black decade of imploring, suing, marching, lobbying, singing, rebelling, praying, and dying we had come to this: a Vice-Presidential Dixie with the President as his straight man. In the serious and <u>frivolous</u> places of power—at the end of that decade—America was still virtually lily-white. And most of the people in that room were reveling in it. What, I wondered, would it take for them to understand that men also come in colors other than white. Seeing and feeling their blindness, I shuddered at the answers that came most readily to mind.

13 As we stood voluntarily, some more slowly than others, when the two men began to play "God Bless America," I couldn't help remembering Judy Collins (who could not sing in Chicago) singing "Where Have All the Flowers Gone?"

14 So later, I joined Nick Kotz, author of "Let Them Eat Promises," and we drank down our dreams.

15 I don't believe that I have been blanketed in and suffocated by such racism and insensitivity since I

was a sophomore in college, when I was the only black invited to a minstrel spoof put on at a white fraternity house.

16 But then, they were only fraternity brothers, weren't they?

Starting Time	
Reading Time	
Finishing Time	
■ Reading Rate	

COMPREHENSION —

Read the following questions and statements. For each one, put an X in the box before the option that contains the most complete or accurate answer.

1. Which of the following famous figures attended the Gridiron Dinner?
   - ☐ a. Lee Iacocca
   - ☐ b. Geraldine Ferraro
   - ☐ c. Ralph Nader
   - ☐ d. Jimmy Stewart

2. This article leads us to believe that
   - ☐ a. journalists and politicians are often racist.
   - ☐ b. racism is an American dream.
   - ☐ c. there will soon be a black president.
   - ☐ d. government is unconsciously sensitive.

3. The facts in the article are presented in
   - ☐ a. order of importance.
   - ☐ b. time order.
   - ☐ c. spatial order.
   - ☐ d. descending order.

4. Which of the following statements best gives the main idea of this selection?
   - ☐ a. The men in the room were full of open prejudice.
   - ☐ b. Because the mayor had been invited, all the insults were forgotten.
   - ☐ c. America is still guilty of insensitivity and racism, conscious and unconscious.
   - ☐ d. It's encouraging to have a president and vice president who can laugh at themselves.

5. The author of this article evidently lives in
   - ☐ a. Boston.
   - ☐ b. Kansas City.
   - ☐ c. New York City.
   - ☐ d. Washington, D.C.

6. The writer of this article makes the judgment that protest over the years had been
   - ☐ a. productive.
   - ☐ b. futile.
   - ☐ c. nonexistent.
   - ☐ d. misplaced.

7. We can infer that many of the jokes that were told at the Gridiron Dinner were
   - ☐ a. political.
   - ☐ b. religious.
   - ☐ c. sexual.
   - ☐ d. racial.

8. The overall tone of this article is
   - ☐ a. hopeful.
   - ☐ b. bitter.
   - ☐ c. loving.
   - ☐ d. funny.

9. The actions of the author at the end of this passage show he is feeling
   - ☐ a. guilty.
   - ☐ b. depressed.
   - ☐ c. satisfied.
   - ☐ d. generous.

10. The setting for the article is
    - ☐ a. a large room.
    - ☐ b. a small courtyard.
    - ☐ c. a large civic center.
    - ☐ d. an outside arena.

Comprehension Skills

1. recalling specific facts
2. retaining concepts
3. organizing facts
4. understanding the main idea
5. drawing a conclusion
6. making a judgment
7. making an inference
8. recognizing tone
9. understanding characters
10. appreciating literary forms

VOCABULARY, PART TWO —

Write the term that makes the most sense in each sentence.

dispirited   **symbiotic**
partisan   **sinister**
frivolous

1. The Gridiron Dinner was not _____; members of both political parties were present.

2. Journalists and politicians fed off each other in a sort of _____ relationship.

3. Everyone at the dinner was in a jolly mood, and so it was not surprising that the entertainment was _____.

4. Wilkins knew the performers essentially meant no harm; nevertheless, he saw something _____ in their acts.

5. He had begun the evening in a happy mood, but now he felt upset and _____.

gross   **montage**
excruciatingly **tangible**
aspirations

6. The performers seemed to insult the hopes and _____ of a generation of blacks.

7. Their bigotry was not subtle; it was so _____ that any intelligent person could recognize it.

8. Photos of their performance would be _____ evidence of their insensitivity.

9. So many photos were taken, in fact, that a _____ of them could be created.

10. As a result of the evening, Wilkins became _____ aware that racism was still a strong element of American society.

Comprehension Score [ ]

Vocabulary Score [ ]

WRITING —

Assume that you are Roger Wilkins. Write a few paragraphs contrasting some specific protest incident from the 1960s with the events at the Gridiron Dinner. Use the same tone in your writing as Wilkins did in this selection.

STUDY SKILLS —

Read the following passage and answer the questions that follow it.

Listening Effectively

A wise man once said that listening is the hardest thing in the world to do. Today, listening is a lost art for most people. Understanding listening faults is a prerequisite to overcoming them. Suggestions for improving listening help you to correct poor habits and cultivate good ones.

Faulty listening leads to misunderstanding, and that can be the cause of many problems. There are those who feel, with good reason, that we might have universal peace if only people would really listen to one another.

In industry, millions of dollars are lost annually as a result of poor listening. Consequently, it has become standard practice at most companies to "write it down."

In school, many students fail to listen properly to instructions. After many exams we hear about those who lose credit because they did not follow directions.

LISTENING FAULTS

One of the causes of faulty listening is daydreaming. This listening fault affects almost everyone. Frequently a speaker will mention some person or thing that triggers an association in our minds and we begin to daydream. When we return to reality and begin listening again, we discover that point three is now being presented and we have no recollection of points one and two.

Opportunities for daydreaming are abundant because people speak at a much slower rate than we can think.

Thus, when a speaker is talking at a rate of 125 words a minute, the listener's mind may wander off.

1. Misunderstanding is caused by

    _____ listening.

2. In _____, poor listening causes

    a loss of millions of dollars annually.

3. In school, students often lose

    _____ in exams as a result of

    poor listening.

4. A speaker will often mention something that will

    trigger an association in our minds and cause us to

    _____.

5. Roger Wilkins certainly had some bad associations in

    his mind when the vice-president sat down at the

    piano and began to play _____.

Showing His True Colors

Angela Bouwsma

AUTHOR NOTES—
Angela Bouwsma had this article published in 1997 in *Newsweek* magazine. She attended the University of California-Berkeley and Georgetown University. Currently she lives in New York City.

VOCABULARY, PART ONE—

All of these terms are in the story you are about to read. Study each term and its meaning. Then answer the questions below.

As you read the story, notice how each term is used. You will have more questions about the terms later.

anonymity, condition where one's identity is not known to others

resorted, turned for help

contrite, sorry; apologetic

restraining order, an order from a judge temporarily forbidding some act until a further ruling is made on it

depicted, portrayed; shown

insidious, happening underneath the surface; sneaky

implicit, meant without being openly stated

chasm, deep gap

mandating, forcing by law

platitude, an empty statement with little meaning

1. Which term could describe a 40-foot-deep ditch down the middle of a street?

   _____

2. Which term could you have used when you wanted to say you were sorry about

   something? _____

3. Which term could identify a statement like "The politicians have your best interests

   at heart"? _____

4. Which term would describe your situation when you attend a meeting and no one

   there knows you? _____

5. Which term might describe a secret plot? _____

A READING PURPOSE—

In this selection Bouwsma presents her case for the need for continuing affirmative action laws. As you read, look for the arguments she uses to make her position convincing to the reader.

1 I was ecstatic when my mother finally turned off the information dirt road and bought a PC a couple of years ago. Last summer she went all out and signed up for America Online. She subscribed because she wanted access to the Internet, not because she wanted to make friends. But as a result of the distinctive name she chose for herself, she often logs on and receives messages from strangers who are intrigued by her AOL handle.

2 Not long ago, my mother told me about a conversation she'd had online with a stranger, a computer engineer from the Midwest. They discussed a variety of topics, and toward the end the subject of beauty came up, followed by race. The man, feeling comfortable after almost an hour of chitchat and not knowing that my mother was black, went on to give her his honest impressions of her kind.

3 She couldn't recall precisely what he said, but the key words were "ignorant," "lie," "cheat" and "smell." My mother, stunned but in the comfort of anonymity, gathered herself and tried to reason with her new friend. He found her efforts to defend black people noble but incredibly naive. "One of these days you'll find out how black people really are," he wrote.

4 With that, my mother gave up reasoning and resorted to the easiest tactic to convince him that

his beliefs were based on ignorance: she revealed that she herself was black. The man professed shock and endlessly apologized. Giving her what I suppose was intended as a compliment, he expressed his happy surprise at finally meeting an intelligent black person.

5 I won't recite my mother's academic and professional accomplishments here. Although her achievements and those of many other black Americans would make her friend look like a sheltered fool as well as a bigot, they're beside the point. The man, relying only on words as clues, assumed my mother was white, someone who would be sympathetic and to whom he could speak freely.

6 What my mother did not ask her computer acquaintance was whether he regarded himself as a racist. He was extremely contrite, even embarrassed, when she revealed her ethnicity. I'll speculate that because he was apologetic and didn't type "You're a lying cheat," he congratulated himself that he'd judged fairly. He might say that his ideas were based on experience. Once he saw how normal she was, the many interests they shared, he was willing to acknowledge her as someone deserving respect.

7 Stories like this have always infuriated me, but my mother's made me sad. She told me that all she could think of as she responded to this intelligent,

college-educated man was me. Her talented, educated daughter, to whom she believed she'd given every advantage, for whom she had so many hopes,

> According to Angela Bouwsma, racism is all around us. It's just not quite as obvious as it used to be.

might be seen on the street by this man and reflexively judged as a stupid, lying cheat.

8   Last November my home state of California abolished affirmative action in state-run agencies and schools. Despite the temporary restraining order issued against it by a federal judge, Proposition 209 scares me a great deal. I'm convinced that, as the mood of the nation dictates, the Supreme Court will uphold it.

9   For a large group of black Americans, particularly those of us trying to make it in corporate America, racism is not experienced the way it's depicted in movies: rednecks brandishing six-packs, bad haircuts and baseball bats. It's better explained by the absence of minorities in certain areas of life—boardrooms, film directors' chairs or editors' desks. In these instances, black Americans are generally denied the opportunity to participate—with a few heralded exceptions—where they are not explicitly required. That kind of racism is subtle and insidious, not something that can be photographed, like a corpse swinging from a tree or a burning cross. It's a racism that smiles at you, shakes your hand, wishes you luck. But its effects are clear and measurable.

10   To say that affirmative action should be scrapped because racial preferences are ideologically intolerable is alarming and insulting. It spits in the face of the reality we all share, one where implicit racial—and gender—preferences not only exist but, at the highest echelons, are the rule of thumb. As a result, more often than not, being black or being a woman pulls a little farther from your reach the top levels of success.

11   So I'm waiting for someone to point out to California Gov. Pete Wilson et al. that there is a chasm of difference between legislating that one not do something and mandating that one do something else. Telling people that they can't hang a NO COLORED NEED APPLY sign outside the executive lounge is not the same thing as forcing them to see to it that a reasonable number of qualified minorities and women get through the door.

12   I am preparing myself for the day the court proclaims that the sun revolves around the earth: that because of the "equal protection before the law" afforded them by the 14th Amendment, minorities and women are not handicapped by entrenched racism and sexism. And as these groups enjoy the same access to opportunity as white males, affirmative action should thereby be discarded. I'm bracing myself for the moment the justices wipe out the only effective—though often misused—method we've come up with to ensure that equal opportunity is not just a lovely, shining platitude but an ethic whose essence Americans can plainly see reflected in their schools and work force.

13   If that happens we'll begin a slide backward after 130 years of slow, painful progress. Such a decision will further polarize us into two separate Americas, one in which racism effectively disappeared the day the Civil Rights Act was signed, and another where it is as much a part of life as breathing. And though I'll urge her to pursue whatever success she desires, as I do, I'll be wondering whether strangers are dismissing *my* daughter the way my mother wonders today.

Starting Time	
Reading Time	
Finishing Time	
Reading Rate	

COMPREHENSION —

Read the following questions and statements. For each one, put an X in the box before the option that contains the most complete or accurate answer.

1. The man Bouwsma's mother was talking to on the Internet was
   - ☐ a. a lawyer.
   - ☐ b. a computer engineer.
   - ☐ c. a truck driver.
   - ☐ d. a teacher.

2. Bouwsma mentions "rednecks brandishing six-packs" in order to
   - ☐ a. describe today's type of racism.
   - ☐ b. describe the man her mother talked to on the Internet.
   - ☐ c. make the point that racism hasn't changed over the years.
   - ☐ d. establish a contrast with today's type of racism.

3. Bouwsma's article used the following organizational plan:
   - ☐ a. an anecdote followed by an argument based on it.
   - ☐ b. a narrative told in chronological order.
   - ☐ c. a narrative using a flashback for effect.
   - ☐ d. a series of comparisons and contrasts.

4. The main point Bouwsma is making is that
   - ☐ a. people are as openly bigoted as ever.
   - ☐ b. affirmative action is still needed.
   - ☐ c. blacks still can't get good jobs.
   - ☐ d. the Supreme Court doesn't have blacks' best interests at heart.

5. Bouwsma believes that affirmative action is needed
   - ☐ a. to right past wrongs.
   - ☐ b. to even things out for whites who have been unfairly left out.
   - ☐ c. to give blacks a chance to get good jobs.
   - ☐ d. to keep poor people in the cities from rioting.

6. The story about the bigoted man on the Internet is intended to
   - ☐ a. embarrass white readers.
   - ☐ b. show that racism is not dead.
   - ☐ c. prove that the man is a redneck.
   - ☐ d. create sympathy for Bouwsma's mother.

7. Bouwsma's family seems to be
   - ☐ a. poor.
   - ☐ b. fairly well off.
   - ☐ c. country people.
   - ☐ d. city people.

8. Bouwsma presents her ideas in a tone that is
   - ☐ a. angry but sympathetic.
   - ☐ b. infuriated and raging.
   - ☐ c. depressed and despairing.
   - ☐ d. upset but controlled.

9. Bouwsma's mother is portrayed as
   - ☐ a. cultured and well-educated.
   - ☐ b. determined to make a better life for herself.
   - ☐ c. shy when talking to strangers.
   - ☐ d. angry and militant.

10. When Bouwsma talks of "racism that smiles at you, shakes your hand, wishes you luck," she is using
   - ☐ a. personification.
   - ☐ b. symbolism.
   - ☐ c. a simile.
   - ☐ d. a literal comparison.

Comprehension Skills
1. recalling specific facts
2. retaining concepts
3. organizing facts
4. understanding the main idea
5. drawing a conclusion
6. making a judgment
7. making an inference
8. recognizing tone
9. understanding characters
10. appreciating literary forms

VOCABULARY, PART TWO —

Write the term that makes the most sense in each sentence.

resorted   contrite
anonymity   depicted
implicit

1. The _____ of speaking on the Internet kept Bouwsma's mother's correspondent from knowing that she was black.

2. The comments the man made about blacks _____ them as stupid, dishonest, and untruthful.

3. Far from being _____ , his racial views were declared outright.

4. When he found out the truth, he _____ to expressions of embarrassment and apology.

5. It was hard to know if he was really _____ or if he only pretended to be sorry.

insidious   **platitude**
chasm   **mandating**
restraining order

6. The only reason the anti-affirmative action law didn't go into effect was because a judge issued a(n) _____.

7. Bouwsma believes there is a deep _____ between opportunities for blacks and opportunities for whites.

8. The difference between racism now and in the past is that whereas before it was out in the open, now it is more underhanded and _____.

9. Bouwsma thinks that for many employers the statement that all people deserve equal opportunity is only a _____.

10. She believes that only by _____ affirmative action will whites be forced to treat blacks equally in the workplace.

Comprehension Score [ ]

Vocabulary Score [ ]

WRITING —

In your opinion, is the sort of racism Bouwsma describes better or worse than the open kind she might have seen 20 or 30 years ago? Take a stand on this question. Write a few paragraphs that defend your position. Use your own personal experiences or those of people you know to support your position.

STUDY SKILLS —

Read the following passage and answer the questions that follow it.

Listening Faults

Here are some faults that will make your listening less effective than it should be.

1. Closed-mindedness. We often refuse to listen to ideas and viewpoints that are contrary to our preconceived notions about a subject. We say, in effect, "I know all I want to know, so there's no use listening."

Actually, this is an intellectual fault that leads to a listening problem. Closed-mindedness interferes with learning by causing you to shut out facts you need to know— whether you agree with them or not.

2. False Attention. This a protective device that everyone resorts to from time to time. When we're not really interested in what a person has to say, we just pretend to listen. We nod and make occasional meaningless comments to give the impression that we are paying attention, when actually our minds are elsewhere.

3. Intellectual Despair. Listening can be difficult at times. Often you must sit through lectures on subjects that are hard to understand.

Obviously, you'll never understand if you give up. The thing to do is to listen more carefully than ever; ask questions when practical and, most important, discuss the material with a classmate. Attack the problem as soon as it appears. Catch up promptly and you'll feel less inclined to adopt an attitude of futility.

4. Personality Listening. It is only natural for listeners to appraise and evaluate a speaker. Our impressions should not interfere with our listening, however. The content must be judged on its own merits.

1. _____ interferes with learning by causing you to shut out facts that you don't agree with.

2. False _____ is a protective device that we all use at one time or another.

3. If you do not understand something from a lecture, it is a good idea to _____ the material with a classmate.

4. The speaker is less important than the _____ of the speech.

5. For example, if you heard Angela Bouwsma presenting the views she discusses in this story, you should agree or _____ on the basis of what she says, not on how she looks.

The Dark Child

Camara Laye

AUTHOR NOTES—

Camara Laye was one of the first writers from sub-Saharan Africa to achieve an international reputation as an author. He was born in French Guinea (now Guinea) in 1928 and lived a portion of his life in Paris. It was there that he wrote his first book, *The Dark Child*, as well as a second one, *The Radiance of the King*, about the journey of a white man through Africa on the way to request an audience with a local king. Laye also wrote numerous short stories and, in 1966, a sequel to *The Dark Child* called *A Dream of Africa*. He died in Senegal in 1980.

VOCABULARY, PART ONE—

All of these terms are in the story you are about to read. Study each term and its meaning. Then answer the questions below.

As you read the story, notice how each term is used. You will have more questions about the terms later.

supplicated, prayed to

swath, a row of grass, grain, or rice

retained, kept; held on to

inviolability, sacredness; quality of not being able to be disturbed or injured

spirited, lively; energetic

crescendo, a gradual increase in loudness

radiant, shining brightly

ecstatically, in an extremely happy way

profusion, a great abundance

permeate, to spread through the whole of

1. Which term might you use in talking about a large quantity of something?

   _____

2. Which term could describe a conversation in which everyone spoke enthusiastically and with energy? _____

3. Which term could be used in describing the light of the sun?

   _____

4. Which term describes something you could cut with a machete?

   _____

5. Which term could describe the action of a person who saved his or her program from a graduation or concert? _____

A R E A D I N G P U R P O S E —

In this selection Laye describes an annual African ritual. As you read, look for details
that make the description come alive.

■

1 December, dry and beautiful, the season of the rice harvest, always found me at Tindican, for this was the occasion of a splendid and joyful festival, to which I was always in invited, and I would impatiently wait for my young uncle to come for me. The festival had no set date, since it awaited the ripening of the rice, and this, in turn, depended on the good will of the weather. Perhaps it depended still more on the good will of the genii of the soil, whom it was necessary to consult. If their reply was favorable, the genii, on the day before the harvest, were again supplicated to provide a clear sky and protection for the reapers, who would be in danger of snakebite.

2 On the day of the harvest, the head of each family went at dawn to cut the first swath in his field. As soon as the first fruits had been gathered, the tom-tom signaled that the harvest had begun. This was the custom; I could not have said then why it was kept and why the signal was only given after the cutting of a swath from each field. I knew that it was customary and inquired no further. Yet, like all our customs, this one had its significance, which I could have discovered by asking the old villagers who retained this kind of knowledge deep in their hearts and memories. But I was not old enough nor curious enough to inquire, nor did I become so until I was no longer in Africa.

3 Today I am inclined to believe that these first swaths destroyed the inviolability of the fields. I do not remember that the reaping went in any particular direction, or if any offerings were made to the genii. Sometimes only the spirit of a tradition survives; sometimes only its form. Its outer garments, as it were, remain. Was that what was involved here? I can not say. Although my visits to Tindican were frequent, I never stayed long enough to acquire a thorough knowledge of all that went on there. All I know is that the tom-tom sounded only after the first fruits had been gathered, and that we eagerly awaited the signal because we wanted to begin the work and escape into the refreshing shade of the great trees and the biting air of the dawn.

4 Once the signal had been given, the reapers set out With them, I marched along to the rhythm of the tom-tom. The young men threw their sickles into the air and caught them as they fell. They shouted simply for the pleasure of shouting, and danced as they followed the tom-tom players. I suppose it would have been wise to heed my grandmother's advice. She had warned me not to be too friendly with these players. But it would have been impossible for me to have torn myself away from their spirited music, from their sickles flashing in the rising sun, from the sweetness of the air and the crescendo of the tom-toms.

110

5 The season itself would not permit it. In December, everything is in flower. Everything is young. Spring and summer seem inseparable and, everywhere,

> Every year the rice had to be harvested. And every year the harvest ritual was repeated.

the country, which, until now has been drenched with rain and dulled by heavy clouds, lies <u>radiant</u>. The sky has never been clearer nor brighter. Birds sing <u>ecstatically</u>. Joy is everywhere, erupts everywhere, and every heart is moved by it. This season, this beautiful season, stirred me deeply. And so did the tom-tom and the festal air that our march acquired. It was a beautiful season, and everything in it—what wasn't there in it? what didn't it pour forth in profusion?—delighted me.

6 When they had reached the first field, the men lined up at the edge, naked to the loins, their sickles ready. My uncle Lansana or some other farmer—for the harvest threw people together and everyone helped everyone else—would signal that the work was to begin. Immediately, the black torsos would bend over the great golden field, and the sickles begin to cut. Now it was not only the morning breeze which made the field tremble, but also the men working.

7 The movement of the sickles as they rose and fell was astonishingly rapid and regular. They had to cut off the stalk between the last joint and the last leaf at the same time that they stripped the leaf. They almost never missed. This was largely due to the way the reaper held the stalks so as to cut them. Nonetheless, the speed of the sickle was astonishing. Each man made it a point of honor to reap as regularly and as rapidly as possible. As he moved across the field he had a bundle of stalks in his hand. His fellows judged him by the number and size of those bundles.

8 My young uncle was wonderful at rice-cutting, the very best. I followed him proudly, step by step, he handing me the bundles of stalks as he cut them. I tore off the leaves, trimmed the stalks, and piled them. Since rice is always harvested when it is very ripe, and, if handled roughly the grains drop off, I had to be very careful. Tying the bundles into sheaves was man's work, but, when they had been tied, I was allowed to put them on the pile in the middle of the field.

9 As the morning drew on, it became hotter. The air seemed to shimmer in a thick haze which was composed of a fine veil of dust from the trampled sod and the stubble. My uncle would wipe the sweat from his chest and forehead and ask for his water-jug. I would run to fetch it from under the leaves where it lay, fresh and cool, and would bring it to him.

10 "Be sure to leave some for me," I would remind him.

11 "Don't worry; I won't drink all of it."

12 He would take great swallows without touching the jug to his lips. "There now. That's better," he would say, handing me the jug. "This dust is sticking in my throat."

13 I would touch my lips to the jug, and immediately the freshness of the water would <u>permeate</u> my body. But refreshment was only momentary, for it passed quickly and left me covered with sweat.

14 "Take your shirt off," my uncle would say. "You're soaking wet. You shouldn't keep wet things on your chest."

15 And he set to work again, and once again I followed him, proud to see that we were ahead of the others.

16 "Aren't you getting tired?" I would ask him.

17 "Why should I be tired?"

18 "Your sickle moves so quickly."

19 "It does, doesn't it?"

20 "We're ahead of the rest."

21 "Yes?"

22 "You know we are. Why do you question it?"

23 "One shouldn't boast."

24 "No."

25 And I would ask myself if someday I would be able to do as well.

Starting Time [   ]

Reading Time [   ]

Finishing Time [   ]

■ Reading Rate [   ]

COMPREHENSION —

Read the following questions and statements. For each one, put an X in the box before the option that contains the most complete or accurate answer.

1. This story takes place in
   - ☐ a. December.
   - ☐ b. October.
   - ☐ c. August.
   - ☐ d. June.

2. The cutting of the first swath
   - ☐ a. was a sacred symbol to the people.
   - ☐ b. had a significance known by only a few.
   - ☐ c. had to be done by the youngest children in the village.
   - ☐ d. came immediately after the sound of the tom-tom.

3. This story is told
   - ☐ a. in strict time order.
   - ☐ b. in spatial order.
   - ☐ c. as a series of examples and supporting arguments.
   - ☐ d. in time order but with some digressions.

4. An appropriate title for this selection would be
   - ☐ a. My Life with My Uncle.
   - ☐ b. The Steps in a Rice Harvest.
   - ☐ c. From Spring to Summer.
   - ☐ d. A Recollection from the Past.

5. At the time of this story, the narrator is
   - ☐ a. a young adult.
   - ☐ b. a teenager.
   - ☐ c. a young boy.
   - ☐ d. a community leader.

6. The narrator's purpose in the selection is to
   - ☐ a. re-create the mood and feel of an event.
   - ☐ b. show how important it is to have elders that one can look up to.
   - ☐ c. show the competition among the harvesters.
   - ☐ d. make clear what a peaceful place Africa is.

7. The narrator would actively participate in the harvest
   - ☐ a. as soon as he got old enough.
   - ☐ b. in the year he is describing and for many years thereafter.
   - ☐ c. never.
   - ☐ d. every few years.

8. Camara Laye's tone in this selection can best be described as
   - ☐ a. sad.
   - ☐ b. humorous.
   - ☐ c. lonely.
   - ☐ d. nostalgic.

9. The narrator's uncle is presented as
   - ☐ a. a strong, confident worker.
   - ☐ b. a strong, boastful worker.
   - ☐ c. a man with little patience for his nephew.
   - ☐ d. a leader in everything he did.

10. The type of work that this selection is taken from is a(n)
    - ☐ a. novel.
    - ☐ b. news article.
    - ☐ c. biography.
    - ☐ d. autobiography.

Comprehension Skills

1. recalling specific facts
2. retaining concepts
3. organizing facts
4. understanding the main idea
5. drawing a conclusion
6. making a judgment
7. making an inference
8. recognizing tone
9. understanding characters
10. appreciating literary forms

VOCABULARY, PART TWO —

Write the term that makes the most sense in each sentence.

swath   inviolability
spirited   profusion
supplicated

1. For as far as the eye could see a great

   _____ of rice was growing.

2. Looking at the rice, the narrator recognized that it

   had a(n) _____ that needed to

   be protected.

112

3. The villagers had _____ the gods for good weather for the rice-cutting ritual.

4. Cutting the first _____ of the rice was the job of the head of each family.

5. The narrator enjoyed the _____ conversation of his relatives at this time of year; it seemed that they were always lively and filled with energy.

retained	**ecstatically**
radiant	**crescendo**
permeate	

6. Rice cutting was such an important ritual that it seemed even the light of the sun was more _____ than usual.

7. People never lost their reverence for the ceremony; they _____ it year after year.

8. The children were so happy that they ran around screaming _____.

9. Their voices reached a _____ as they got more and more excited.

10. A feeling of fulfillment seemed to _____ the entire village.

Comprehension Score	
Vocabulary Score	

WRITING —

Think of a season that holds special appeal for you, as the harvest season did for Camara Laye. Then write a few paragraphs describing your sensual impressions of that season—the things you see, hear, smell, taste, and touch. Try to make the season come alive for your audience.

STUDY SKILLS —

Read the following passage and answer the questions that follow it.

Good Listening, I

To help improve your listening habits, here are some positive steps you can take.

Prepare to Listen. Your attitude while attending class is important. If you feel that a particular class is a waste of time, you obviously will not be in the mood to listen. It is difficult and almost impossible to get anything out of a lecture that you are not prepared for. To prepare, decide before class that the lecture period will be well spent; resolve to make it a learning experience.

Another good way to prepare for a lecture is to keep ahead in your textbook and other required reading. The more you know about a subject in advance, the more interested you will be in hearing what the instructor has to say about it. For prepared students lectures become an exchange of ideas rather than a deluge of unfamiliar and seemingly unrelated facts.

Watch the Speaker. Don't take your eyes off the speaker. When you look away, you invite visual distractions that may compete for your attention. In class you must listen with your eyes as well as with your ears.

Develop an awareness of the speaker's mannerisms. The gestures a speaker makes supplement his remarks. What a writer does with punctuation, bold print, headlines, and italics, a speaker does with vocal inflection and body gestures. All speakers communicate physically as well as orally. You must watch as you listen.

1. It is important to attend class with a good _____.

2. You will be more interested in the subject of the lecture if you read about it in _____.

3. For example, if you had read Laye's story before your instructor lectured about it, you would have known that the event it describes is a _____.

4. In class you must listen with your

    _____ as well as with your ears.

5. The speaker's _____ supplement

    his remarks.

The Harlem Rat

John H. Jones

AUTHOR NOTES—

"The Harlem Rat" was featured in *Harlem, U.S.A.*, a collection of stories that take place in Harlem, a predominantly black section of New York City. The collection, published in 1964, was edited by John Henrik Clarke.

VOCABULARY, PART ONE—

All of these terms are in the story you are about to read. Study each term and its meaning. Then answer the questions below.

As you read the story, notice how each term is used. You will have more questions about the terms later.

priority, precedence or preference

stalked, walked with slow, stiff strides

staccato, irregular, with breaks in between

contemplating, thinking over carefully

imply, to suggest without saying directly

glowered, stared with a threatening expression

sluggishly, slowly; lazily

predicament, puzzling or difficult situation

suppressed, withheld

agonizing, distressing; heartbreaking

1. Which term could describe a hard-to-deal-with problem?

   _____

2. Which term would describe your action if you held back or hid information that someone wanted? _____

3. Which term describes how a person walked who moved with very little energy?

   _____

4. Which term could identify a situation that you had to deal with before all others?

   _____

5. Which term could describe how someone looked at you if the expression on his or her face frightened you? _____

A READING PURPOSE —

This selection shows how a husband and wife relate to each other in a frustrating situation. Read to see if they are able to find a way out of the situation.

■

1 As Battle Young strode home along Harlem's Lenox Avenue on an October evening in nineteen-forty-eight, he scarcely noticed the chilly wind or the passersby. He was too absorbed in his own anger.

2 He swung a lunch pail as he walked, a tall, lithe man in Army clothes, thick-soled boots, khaki trench coat and knitted cap. His brown face was strong-featured, and his brown eyes mirrored an eternal hurt, frustration or anger. He was a veteran, discharged only a year, after three bitter ones in the Army.

3 Crossing One Hundred and Thirty-fifth Street and heading north, his mind searched for the easiest way to tell Belle that he had failed to again get an apartment in the new project going up on Fifth Avenue. He thought of how she wanted to get out of those dismal three rooms on One Hundred and Thirty-eighth Street, so that Jean, their two-month-old baby, would have "a decent place to grow up in."

4 Belle had cried, threatened, pleaded, scolded, ridiculed and tried just about everything else in what she thought was the best method to make him get out and find a place! "Other vets are finding places. Why can't you?" she would cry out whenever she heard of someone else getting an apartment.

5 "We're lucky to find this hole." He told her over and over again, explaining that he wanted to get another place the same as she did. But she had always been a demanding woman, he thought, remembering

their school days in Richmond, Virginia. It had been her strong persuasion after his Army discharge that brought them to New York.

6 And then, when the city-owned project started up giving priority to veterans, Belle had been certain they would get in. But just this evening he'd stood in line for an hour, only to have the interviewer tell him, "You're making too much money, Mr. Young. Your income is about three dollars a week more than the law calls for." He had argued at first and finally stalked out in anger. And now he had to face another one of those terrible arguments with Belle. God! How he hated to fight with her!

7 He walked around an unconscious Sneaky Pete drinker sprawled on the sidewalk at One Hundred and Thirty-sixth Street, crossed and glanced toward the Harlem Hospital as an ambulance turned east. Well, he had to go home, he thought, walking on in silence, swinging his lunch pail and staring in through the windows of the bars, the greasy cafes and the candy stores.

8 At the corner of One Hundred and Thirty-eighth Street, he turned east, walked past two tenements and entered the third. On the stoop stood a half dozen teen-age boys and girls. Climbing two flights of creaky stairs, he stopped just at the top of the landing, put his key in the lock and went in the door.

9 Belle could see the answer in his grimy face when he came in, but she asked the question anyway,

asked it hopefully, standing in the middle of the front room. "What did they say at the project, honey?" Her voice was soft but clear.

> Battle Young endured as best he could the crumbling ceilings, the cold water, even the roaches. Then came the final indignity.

10 "For Crissakes! Will you let me outta these dirty clothes and catch a breath?" he snapped, and then turned away ashamed.

11 Belle took the pail from his hands, turned on her heel and walked into the middle room. She was slender, and her skin was a delicate reddish tan. Her brown hair was held up neatly by a hair net. Brown eyes accented a snub nose and soft, full, unpainted lips. She wore a blue and red flowered house dress, and fuzzy blue slippers.

12 The small room was dimly lit. On an old-fashioned iron bed in the corner a tiny baby slept. This was Jean. Belle smiled anxiously as she peered at the baby. Satisfied that Jean was snug, she turned and inspected the small, round, black oil stove. The flame glowed through the vents in its side.

13 Belle shivered slightly, turned it up and silently cursed Kelly, the landlord, for not providing heat.

14 The ceilings were cracked and falling. The dirty gray plaster walls appeared to have once been buff. Ancient chandeliers had become loosened from the ceiling, and from time to time the crumbling electric wire insulation wore through and short-circuited, plunging the apartment into darkness.

15 Going down a short hall, Belle mashed a roach with her foot as it scurried across the floor heading for the kitchen. She put Battle's pail on the top of a wooden icebox standing in a far corner and went to her stove. After half an hour, Battle came in wearing a tattered blue terrycloth bathrobe. His stiff, black hair was cropped short, and he carried an evening paper. His face, now clean, wore an annoyed expression as he walked to a cracked, porcelain-topped table, pulled out a rickety chair and sat down with a sigh. He glanced at the paper's headlines while Belle stirred a pot. Both looked up knowingly as the steam pipe clanged a <u>staccato</u> beat of an overhead tenant calling for heat.

16 "That damn water is cold again. The day I leave this filthy hole I'm gonna kick that lousy Kelly right in his can!" Battle stormed. "Ain't no need of sayin' anything to the super. Kelly won't give him no coal!"

17 "Again?" Belle commented with sarcasm. "It's always cold." Then, "What did they say, honey?" She reached back on the table for Battle's plate.

18 "I'm making too much," Battle said, looking hopefully as Belle dished up a sizzling pork chop, steaming lima beans, and kale.

19 Belle exclaimed, pushing the plate of food before Battle. "Whadda they mean? You making too much. We can hardly buy bread and meat!"

20 Battle chewed a mouthful and swallowed. "Well, there's this law against a guy making more than thirty-six dollars getting in city housing projects."

21 "Did you show 'em your discharge papers and tell 'em about me and Jean?"

22 "Sure. But that don't mean nothing."

23 "Well, since we got to stay here why don't you try to make Kelly fix up a few things and paint?" Belle said as she sat down to her own plate of food.

24 Battle slammed down his fork, and looked Belle straight in the eyes. "Now don't you go nagging at me again. Haven't I cussed and threatened ever since we been here? And Brown in 1-E was here long before us, and Kelly ain't done anything in his apartment yet!" He picked up the fork, speared a piece of meat and started chewing savagely.

25 But Belle wasn't satisfied. She pushed the food about her plate without interest, <u>contemplating</u> an appropriate reply. "Well, can't you think of anything else? Can't you go see somebody? Isn't there a law for his kind? Or do you want me to do it?"

26 Battle had heard this before. She always managed to <u>imply</u> doubts of his ability to do things the way a man should, hitting his weakest spot. "Look," he muttered through a mouthful of food, "do you want me to kill that bastard, and go to Sing Sing? 'Cause if I get into one more argument with him and he gets smart, I'm gonna hit him with the first thing I get my hands on!"

27 "Fighting won't get the place painted, but thinking out a few ways to make him do it might help a little!" she blazed. She hesitated a moment. "You never did go back to that tenants' meeting, like Mr. Brown asked you to. You and the rest of these folks ought to listen to Mr. Brown and get together. You can't do nothing by yourselves."

28 Battle <u>glowered</u> and broke off a bit of white bread. For a few minutes they both ate in silence. Noticing that Battle was almost finished with his food, Belle said, "There's no more meat or beans, just kale, but there's some rice pudding from yesterday, and—"

29 Battle sputtered suddenly, staring at the wall against which the table stood. A fat roach <u>sluggishly</u>

made its way ceiling-wards, antennae waving.

30 "Well, knock him off for heavensake, and stop cussing!"

31 He reached down, pulled off a battered bedroom slipper and unceremoniously smashed the roach. They both looked disgustedly at the mess. Then, as Belle got up and turned toward the icebox, Battle tore a corner from the newspaper he had been reading and wiped the wall.

32 "I don't want any pudding now, " he said just before she stooped to open the box.

33 "Well, why did you mash him, Mister nice-nasty?" She came back to the table, sat down, and pulled a pack of cigarettes from her dress pocket. Battle pushed his dishes back and continued to read.

34 Belle lit her cigarette and blew out the first puff. Her mind was busy trying to hit on the best way to mention their housing predicament again. Battle seemed to sense her thoughts, and he glanced at her from the corners of his eyes several times. "Honey—" she began. Battle stiffened physically and mentally, but he turned to the sport page as though he hadn't heard.

35 This always annoyed Belle. She reached over and snatched the paper from him. "I'm talking to you, man! If you don't get me and my baby outta this rat trap, I will!"

36 Battle suppressed a desire to shout back. Instead he just stared at her and then reached patiently for the paper. She jerked it out of his reach. "You can sit there like a knot on a log if you want to!" Belle blazed.

37 A whimper from the baby in the middle room went unheard by either of them. Battle raised himself half out of the chair, reached over and grabbed Belle's arm, twisting it, and pulled the paper loose. She began to scratch at him but stopped abruptly when an agonizing cry came from the baby. She released the paper, jumped up and ran from the kitchen. The baby still shrieked while Battle shuffled the crumpled pages back into place.

38 "My God, Battle! Come here! It's a rat!"

39 As he dashed into the room, Belle held Jean in one arm, and inspected two rows of teeth marks on the baby's right cheek. Blood oozed from each mark.

40 "He bit her, Battle! Oh God! He bit her!" she wailed as her husband rushed in.

41 As Battle looked at the tiny blobs of blood, smothering anger arose.

42 "Better go and put some iodine on her," he told Belle.

43 He spun at a noise under the bed, and stomped viciously as a dirty gray rat the size of a kitten scampered across the room.

44 Gritting his teeth he looked into the bathroom where Belle painted Jean's bites.

45 "How late does Kelly stay in his office?" he asked so quietly it alarmed Belle.

46 "Eight. What you gonna do, Battle? Don't get into no trouble!"

47 "I ain't gonna start no fighting trouble, but I'm gonna make it hot for Kelly."

48 He went back in the room, opened a closet and pulled on his clothes. He glanced at a clock on a dresser that said seven-thirty P.M. He went back to the bathroom door.

49 "Then tomorrow I'm gonna go from door to door and tell everybody in the tenant council what happened."

50 Belle smiled as he kissed her lightly, and patted Jean's head.

51 He left and went to see the landlord. ∎

Starting Time [ ]

Reading Time [ ]

Finishing Time [ ]

Reading Rate [ ]

COMPREHENSION —
Read the following questions and statements. For each one, put an X in the box before the option that contains the most complete or accurate answer.

1. This story takes place in
   - ☐ a. 1942.
   - ☐ b. 1944.
   - ☐ c. 1946.
   - ☐ d. 1948.

2. Belle tried to prod her husband to action by
   - ☐ a. complaining to the landlord.
   - ☐ b. attacking his manhood.
   - ☐ c. joining the neighborhood council.
   - ☐ d. looking for a job.

3. This story is told, using
   - ☐ a. simple listing.
   - ☐ b. time order.
   - ☐ c. spatial development.
   - ☐ d. cause and effect.

4. The Harlem rat of the title is
   - ☐ a. Battle.
   - ☐ b. the interviewer.
   - ☐ c. Kelly.
   - ☐ d. Belle.

5. After Jean was bitten by the rat, Battle
   - ☐ a. attacked Kelly.
   - ☐ b. became an activist.
   - ☐ c. hounded Belle.
   - ☐ d. packed his belongings.

6. Which of the following best reflects Belle's thinking?
   - ☐ a. Honest poverty hath no shame.
   - ☐ b. The squeaky door is the one that gets oil.
   - ☐ c. Problems are best resolved at home.
   - ☐ d. Tomorrow is another day.

7. Battle refused the rice pudding because
   - ☐ a. he had had enough to eat.
   - ☐ b. he did not like desserts.
   - ☐ c. he had lost his appetite.
   - ☐ d. it was stale.

8. The tone of the selection is one of
   - ☐ a. wishful thinking.
   - ☐ b. fearful anxiety.
   - ☐ c. depressing futility.
   - ☐ d. deliberate oppression.

9. Belle can be described as
   - ☐ a. a shrewish wife.
   - ☐ b. hopelessly dejected.
   - ☐ c. a careless housekeeper.
   - ☐ d. impatient and frustrated.

10. The author develops the relationship between Belle and Battle by using
    - ☐ a. description.
    - ☐ b. comparison.
    - ☐ c. dialogue.
    - ☐ d. facts.

Comprehension Skills
1. recalling specific facts
2. retaining concepts
3. organizing facts
4. understanding the main idea
5. drawing a conclusion
6. making a judgment
7. making an inference
8. recognizing tone
9. understanding characters
10. appreciating literary forms

VOCABULARY, PART TWO —
Write the term that makes the most sense in each sentence.

priority   **stalked**
glowered   **predicament**
suppressed

1. When Battle _____ at her, Belle could see the anger in his face.

2. Often Battle's frustration showed as he _____ back and forth in the apartment.

3. Neither Belle's nor Battle's anger was _____ much any more; they came right out and expressed their feelings.

4. Living in a dismal apartment but not being able to find another was a terrible _____ for Battle.

119

5. Belle thought that his first _____,
   before anything else, should be to get them out
   of there.

staccato   **contemplating**
imply   **sluggishly**
agonizing

6. Though she didn't come right out and say it,
   sometimes a comment from Belle would
   _____ that Battle was less
   than a man.

7. Battle sat quietly, _____ with
   great concentration what he should do.

8. Only the _____ sound of an-
   other tenant periodically beating on the pipes
   broke the silence.

9. It was _____ to see the marks
   where the rat had bitten the baby; Battle could almost have cried.

10. The fact that cockroaches moved
    _____ made it easy to kill
    them.

Comprehension Score [ ]

Vocabulary Score [ ]

WRITING —
How would you characterize Battle in this selection? How
sympathetic did you feel toward his efforts to do something for his wife and daughter? Write a few paragraphs
expressing your thoughts and feelings.

STUDY SKILLS —
Read the following passage and answer the questions
that follow it.

Good Listening, II
Note Questions. Listen closely to questions asked in
class. When an instructor asks a question, he or she is
probably about to discuss something important and is
calling for your attention. This is an important signal between a speaker and the listeners.

Speakers' questions are designed to help you listen
and learn. You should also notice questions asked by others in the class. Student questions signal the instructor;
they indicate how the message is coming across. The instructor will elaborate and illustrate, repeat and para-
phrase, to help the listeners understand the matter.
Questions from both teacher and students are valuable;
pay attention to them.

Listen Creatively. You should not think about other
things while listening to a speaker; you must give your
entire attention to the speaker's words.

Ask Questions. If questions are not permitted during
a class session, write yours in your notebook and get the
answers later.

Bring Questions to Class. Your attention is sharpened
when you are listening for answers. If your instructor
calls for class participation, don't be afraid or shy about
speaking up. Your attention is focused most sharply when
you are on the firing line; and if you are mistaken and
are corrected in class, you won't be likely to forget the
correct response at exam time.

Your success in school will depend largely on how well
you listen in class. If applied, the suggestions offered
here can substantially improve your ability in this vital
area.

1. Instructors use questions as a way to call for
   _____.

2. When you listen, do not _____
   about other things.

3. Your attention is sharpened when you are
   _____ for answers.

4. If you are mistaken and corrected in class, you will
   not _____ the correct response
   later.

5. For example, if you mistakenly answered that the
   Harlem _____ was Battle, the
   right answer would probably stick in your mind come
   exam time.

BIBLIOGRAPHY

Angelou, Maya. *I Know Why the Caged Bird Sings*. New York: Random House, 1969.

Archer, Chalmers, Jr. *Growing Up Black in Rural Mississippi*. New York: Walker and Company, 1992.

Baldwin, James. "Sweet Lorraine." In *To Be Young, Gifted, and Black*. New Jersey: Prentice-Hall, 1969.

Bambara, Toni Cade. "The Pill: Genocide or Liberation." In *Onyx*. New York: Onyx Publications, 1969.

Baraka, Amiri [LeRoi Jones]. *The Autobiography of LeRoi Jones*. New York: Freundlich Books, 1984.

Blay, J. Benibengor. "Funeral of a Whale." In *An African Treasury*. Edited by Langston Hughes. New York: Crown Publishers, 1960.

Brooks, Gwendolyn. "I love those little booths at Benvenuti's." In *Selected Poems*. New York: HarperCollins, 1963.

Brown, Sterling. "A Century of Negro Portraiture in American Literature." In *Massachusetts Review*. Amherst: University of Massachusetts, 1966.

———. "Children of the Mississippi." In *The Collected Poems of Sterling A. Brown*. Edited by Michael S. Harper. New York: HarperCollins, 1980.

Carmichael, Stokley, and Charles V. Hamilton. *Black Power*. New York: Random House, 1967.

Clarke, John Henrik. "The Boy Who Painted Christ Black." In *American Negro Short Stories*. Edited by John Henrik Clarke. New York: Hill and Wang, 1966.

———. "The Origin and Growth of Afro-American Literature." In *Negro Digest*, Chicago: Johnson Publishing Company, Inc., 1967.

Cosby, Bill. *Fatherhood*. New York: Doubleday & Company, 1986.

———. "How to Win at Basketball: Cheat." In *Look*, January 27, 1970.

Cose, Ellis. *The Rage of a Privileged Class*. New York: Harper-Collins, 1993.

Cullen, Countee. "Thoughts in a Zoo." In *My Soul's High Song*. Edited by Gerald Early. New York: Doubleday, 1991.

Danticat, Edwidge. "New York Day Women." In *Krik? Krak!* New York: Soho Press, 1995.

Davis, Angela. *Women, Race and Class*. New York: Random House, 1981.

Douglass, Frederick. *My Bondage and My Freedom,* 1855.

———. *Narrative of the Life of Frederick Douglass, An American Slave,* 1845.

DuBois, W. E. B. *Dusk of Dawn*. New York: Harcourt, Brace & World, 1968.

Dunham, Katherine. *A Touch of Innocence*. New York: Harcourt Brace Jovanovich, 1959.

Equiano, Olaudah. *Equiano's Travels: The Interesting Narrative of the Life of Olaudah Equiano, or Gustavus Vassa, the African,* 1789.

Farmer, James. *Lay Bare the Heart*. New York: Arbor House, 1985.

Garvey, Marcus. *Philosophy and Opinions,* 1916.

Gates, Henry Louis, Jr. *Colored People*. New York: Alfred A. Knopf, 1994.

Gregory, Dick, and Robert Lipsyte. *nigger, an autobiography*. New York: E. P. Dutton & Co., 1964.

Hansberry, Lorraine. *A Raisin in the Sun*. New York: Random House, 1958.

Hurston, Zora Neale. *Dust Tracks on a Road*. Urbana, Illinois: University of Illinois Press, 1942.

Jackson, Reggie, with Mike Lupica. *Reggie*. New York: Villard Books, 1984.

Johnson, Charles. *Middle Passage*. New York: Penguin, 1990.

King, Martin Luther, Jr. "A View from the Mountaintop." Martin Luther King, Jr. Estate, 1968.

Mandela, Nelson. "Indictment of South Africa." In *The Political Awakening of Africa*. New Jersey: Prentice-Hall, 1965.

Mandela, Winnie. *Part of My Soul Went with Him*. New York: W. W. Norton & Company, 1985.

McMillan, Terry. *Disappearing Acts*. New York: Viking Penguin, 1989.

Modisane, Bloke. "Why I Ran Away." In *An African Treasury*. Edited by Langston Hughes. New York: Crown Publishers, 1960.

Morrison, Toni. *Sula*. New York: Alfred A. Knopf, 1973.

Pemberton, Gayle. *The Hottest Water in Chicago*. Boston: Faber and Faber, 1992.

Reed, Ishmael. "Distant Cousins." In *Airing Dirty Laundry*. Reading, Massachusetts: Addison-Wesley, 1993.

Taulbert, Clifton L. *The Last Train North*. Tulsa: Council Oak Books, 1992.

Walcott, Derek. "The Glory Trumpeter." In *Collected Poems, 1948–1984*. Farrar, Straus & Giroux, 1986

Walker, Alice. "Brothers and Sisters" and "Choice: A Tribute to Dr. Martin Luther King, Jr." In *In Search of Our Mother's Gardens: Womanist Prose*. New York: Harcourt Brace Jovanovich, 1983.

———. *The Color Purple*. New York: Harcourt Brace Jovanovich, 1982.

Walker, Margaret. *Jubilee*. Boston: Houghton Mifflin Company, 1966.

Washington, Booker T. "Atlanta Compromise Speech." In *Up from Slavery: An Autobiography,* 1900.

Wells-Barnett, Ida B. "Lynch Law in All Its Phases," 1893.

Wideman, John Edgar. *Brothers and Keepers*. New York: Henry Holt and Company, 1984.

———. *Fatheralong*. New York: Pantheon, 1994.

Wright, Richard. *Black Boy*. New York: Harper & Brothers, 1945.

Words-per-Minute Table

Selection # words	1	2	3	4	5	6	7	8	9	10	11	12	13	14	15	16	17	18	19	20
	1829	1722	1387	1800	1944	1267	1742	1599	1986	1389	1520	998	1416	1610	1145	1517	1281	1004	1162	1909
1:20	1372	1292	1040	1350	1458	950	1307	1199	1490	1042	1140	749	1062	1208	859	1138	961	753	872	1432
1:40	1097	1033	832	1080	1166	760	1045	959	1192	833	912	599	850	966	687	910	769	602	697	1145
2:00	915	861	694	900	972	634	871	800	993	695	760	499	708	805	573	759	641	502	581	955
2:20	784	738	594	771	833	543	747	685	851	595	651	428	607	690	491	650	549	430	498	818
2:40	686	646	520	675	729	475	653	600	745	521	570	374	531	604	429	569	480	377	436	716
3:00	610	574	462	600	648	422	581	533	662	463	507	333	472	537	382	506	427	335	387	636
3:20	549	517	416	540	583	380	523	480	596	417	456	299	425	483	344	455	384	301	349	573
3:40	499	470	378	491	530	346	475	436	542	379	415	272	386	439	312	414	349	274	317	521
4:00	457	431	347	450	486	317	436	400	497	347	380	250	354	403	286	379	320	251	291	477
4:20	422	397	320	415	449	292	402	369	458	321	351	230	327	372	264	350	296	232	268	441
4:40	392	369	297	386	417	272	373	343	426	298	326	214	303	345	245	325	275	215	249	409
5:00	366	344	277	360	389	253	348	320	397	278	304	200	283	322	229	303	256	201	232	382
5:20	343	323	260	338	365	238	327	300	372	260	285	187	266	302	215	284	240	188	218	358
5:40	323	304	245	318	343	224	307	282	350	245	268	176	250	284	202	268	226	177	205	337
6:00	305	287	231	300	324	211	290	267	331	232	253	166	236	268	191	253	214	167	194	318
6:20	289	272	219	284	307	200	275	252	314	219	240	158	224	254	181	240	202	159	183	301
6:40	274	258	208	270	292	190	261	240	298	208	228	150	212	242	172	228	192	151	174	286
7:00	261	246	198	257	278	181	249	228	284	198	217	143	202	230	164	217	183	143	166	273
7:20	249	235	189	245	265	173	238	218	271	189	207	136	193	220	156	207	175	137	158	260
7:40	239	225	181	235	254	165	227	209	259	181	198	130	185	210	149	198	167	131	152	249
8:00	229	215	173	225	243	158	218	200	248	174	190	125	177	201	143	190	160	126	145	239
8:20	219	207	166	216	233	152	209	192	238	167	182	120	170	193	137	182	154	120	139	229
8:40	211	199	160	208	224	146	201	185	229	160	175	115	163	186	132	175	148	116	134	220
9:00	203	191	154	200	216	141	194	178	221	154	169	111	157	179	127	169	142	112	129	212
9:20	196	185	149	193	208	136	187	171	213	149	163	107	152	173	123	163	137	108	125	205
9:40	189	178	143	186	201	131	180	165	205	144	157	103	146	167	118	157	133	104	120	197
10:00	183	172	139	180	194	127	174	160	199	139	152	100	142	161	115	152	128	100	116	191
10:20	177	167	134	174	188	123	169	155	192	134	147	97	137	156	111	147	124	97	112	185
10:40	171	161	130	169	182	119	163	150	186	130	143	94	133	151	107	142	120	94	109	179
11:00	166	157	126	164	177	115	158	145	181	126	138	91	129	146	104	138	116	91	106	174
11:20	161	152	122	159	172	112	154	141	175	123	134	88	125	142	101	134	113	89	103	168
11:40	157	148	119	154	167	109	149	137	170	119	130	86	121	138	98	130	110	86	100	164
12:00	152	144	116	150	162	106	145	133	166	116	127	83	118	134	95	126	107	84	97	159
12:20	148	140	112	146	158	103	141	130	161	113	123	81	115	131	93	123	104	81	94	155
12:40	144	136	110	142	153	100	138	126	157	110	120	79	112	127	90	120	101	79	92	151
13:00	141	132	107	138	150	97	134	123	153	107	117	77	109	124	88	117	99	77	89	147
13:20	137	129	104	135	146	95	131	120	149	104	114	75	106	121	86	114	96	75	87	143
13:40	134	126	101	132	142	93	127	117	145	102	111	73	104	118	84	111	94	73	85	140
14:00	131	123	99	129	139	91	124	114	142	99	109	71	101	115	82	108	92	72	83	136
14:20	128	120	97	126	136	88	122	112	139	97	106	70	99	112	80	106	89	70	81	133
14:40	125	117	95	123	133	86	119	109	135	95	104	68	97	110	78	103	87	68	79	130
15:00	122	115	92	120	130	84	116	107	132	93	101	67	94	107	76	101	85	67	77	127

Minutes and Seconds Elapsed

Progress Graph

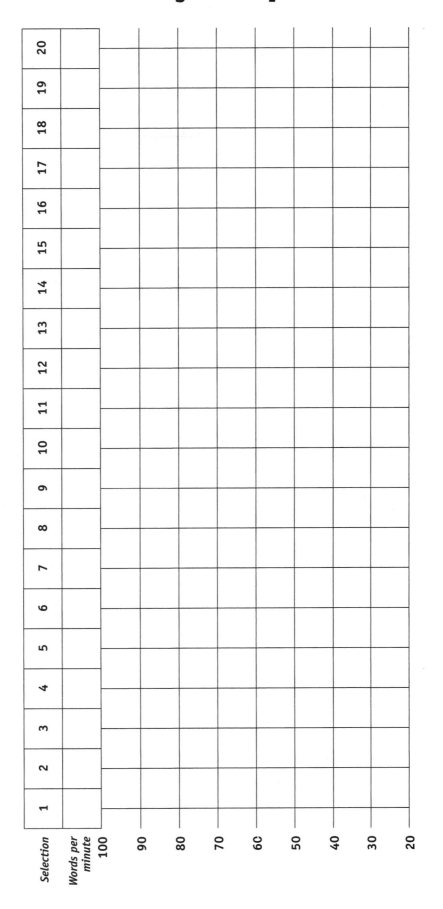

Comprehension Skills Profile

The graph below is designed to help you see your areas of comprehension weakness. Because all the comprehension questions in this text are coded, it is possible for you to determine which kinds of questions give you the most trouble.

On the graph below, keep a record of the questions you have answered incorrectly. Following each selection, darken a square on the graph next to the number of the question missed. The columns are labeled with the selection numbers.

By looking at the chart and noting the number of shaded squares, you should be able to tell which areas of comprehension you are weak in. A large number of shaded squares across from a particular skill signifies an area of reading comprehension weakness. When you discover a particular weakness, give greater attention and time to answering questions of that type.

Further, you might wish to check with your instructor for recommendations of appropriate practice materials.

Categories of Comprehension Skills

Selection	1	2	3	4	5	6	7	8	9	10	11	12	13	14	15	16	17	18	19	20
1. recalling specific facts																				
2. retaining concepts																				
3. organizing facts																				
4. understanding the main idea																				
5. drawing a conclusion																				
6. making a judgment																				
7. making an inference																				
8. recognizing tone																				
9. understanding characters																				
10. appreciating literary forms																				